Recurrent Neural Networks with Python Quick Start Guide

Sequential learning and language modeling with TensorFlow

Simeon Kostadinov

BIRMINGHAM - MUMBAI

Recurrent Neural Networks with Python Quick Start Guide

Commissioning Editor: Amey Varangaonkar
Acquisition Editor: Siddharth Mandal
Content Development Editor: Roshan Kumar
Technical Editor: Sushmeeta Jena
Copy Editor: Safis Editing
Project Coordinator: Hardik Binde
Proofreader: Safis Editing
Indexer: Mariammal Chettiyar
Graphics: Alishon Mendonsa
Production Coordinator: Aparna Bhagat

First published: November 2018

Production reference: 1281118

Published by Packt Publishing Ltd.
Livery Place
35 Livery Street
Birmingham
B3 2PB, UK.

ISBN 978-1-78913-233-5

www.packtpub.com

`mapt.io`

Mapt is an online digital library that gives you full access to over 5,000 books and videos, as well as industry leading tools to help you plan your personal development and advance your career. For more information, please visit our website.

Why subscribe?

- Spend less time learning and more time coding with practical eBooks and Videos from over 4,000 industry professionals

- Improve your learning with Skill Plans built especially for you

- Get a free eBook or video every month

- Mapt is fully searchable

- Copy and paste, print, and bookmark content

Packt.com

Did you know that Packt offers eBook versions of every book published, with PDF and ePub files available? You can upgrade to the eBook version at `www.packt.com` and as a print book customer, you are entitled to a discount on the eBook copy. Get in touch with us at `customercare@packtpub.com` for more details.

At `www.packt.com`, you can also read a collection of free technical articles, sign up for a range of free newsletters, and receive exclusive discounts and offers on Packt books and eBooks.

Contributors

About the author

Simeon Kostadinov is a software engineer and deep learning enthusiast who loves learning while being involved in long-term projects that aim to improve peoples' lives. He is currently in his final year at the University of Birmingham studying computer science. During his studies, he spent a year in San Francisco working with the incredibly smart Speechify team. His programming knowledge includes Swift, Python, and JavaScript. Simeon is also passionate about the field of AI and how it can transform the businesses of today.

I would like to thank my friend, Boyan, for taking the time to review the book so diligently. Also, I want to express my gratitude to my girlfriend, Sofia, for the constant support during my writing.

This book wouldn't have been possible without the help of the whole Packt team, including Roshan, Siddharth, and many more. Finally, I want to thank my friends, Vladimir and Cliff; as well as my brother, Valentin; my mom, Ekaterina; and my dad, Valentin.

About the reviewer

Boyan Bonev is a software engineer and machine learning enthusiast with experience in web and desktop development. He has been an intern for both IBM and CERN and so is highly skilled in C#, JavaScript, Java, Python, Haskell, and various frameworks. He has also been involved in working with teams using different agile techniques. He is very passionate about cognitive technologies that will change the future, which is why he has taken so many Coursera courses. Outside his hobby, he loves spending time with his family and friends. Boyan is also very passionate about helping young adults who have been diagnosed with leukemia.

> *I would like to thank Simeon for his enthusiasm and professionalism in writing this book. I think that he has done a wonderful job. I am more than sure that the way he has done it will be of huge benefit to many people.*

Packt is searching for authors like you

If you're interested in becoming an author for Packt, please visit `authors.packtpub.com` and apply today. We have worked with thousands of developers and tech professionals, just like you, to help them share their insight with the global tech community. You can make a general application, apply for a specific hot topic that we are recruiting an author for, or submit your own idea.

Table of Contents

Preface

Deep learning (DL) is an increasingly popular topic that attracts the attention of the largest corporations as well as that of all kinds of developers. Over the past five years, this field has seen massive improvements that have ultimately led us to think of DL as a highly disruptive technology with immense potential. Virtual assistants, speech recognition, and language translation are just a few examples of the direct implementation of DL techniques. Compared to image recognition or object detection, these applications use sequential data, where the nature of every result depends upon that of the previous one. For example, you can't produce a meaningful translation of a sentence from English to Spanish without tracking the words from beginning to end. For these kinds of problems, a specific type of model is being used—the **recurrent neural network (RNN)**. In this book, we will cover the basics of RNNs and focus on some practical implementations using the popular DL library TensorFlow. All examples are accompanied by in-depth explanations of the theory to help you understand the underlying concepts behind this powerful but slightly complex model. Reading this book will leave you confident in your knowledge of RNNs and give you a good head start in using this model for your own specific use cases.

Who this book is for

This book is for machine learning engineers and data scientists who want to learn about RNNs by looking at practical use cases.

What this book covers

Chapter 1, *Introducing Recurrent Neural Networks*, will provide you with a brief introduction to the basics of RNNs and will compare the model to other popular models and demonstrate why RNNs are the best. This chapter will then illustrate RNNs with the use of an example. You will also be given insight into the problems that RNNs have.

Chapter 2, *Building Your First RNN with TensorFlow*, will explore how to build a simple RNN to solve the problem of identifying sequence parity. You will also gain a brief understanding of the TensorFlow library and how it can be utilized for building DL models. After reading this chapter, you should have a full understanding of how to use TensorFlow with Python and how easy and straightforward it is to build a neural network.

Chapter 3, *Generating Your Own Book Chapter*, will also introduce a new and more powerful RNN model called the **gated recurrent unit** (**GRU**). You will learn how it works and why we are choosing it over the simple RNN. You will also go step by step over the process of generating a book chapter. By the end of this chapter, you should have gained both a theoretical and a practical knowledge that will give you the freedom to experiment with any problems of medium difficulty.

Chapter 4, *Creating a Spanish-to-English Translator*, will walk you through building a fairly sophisticated neural network model using the sequence-to-sequence model implemented with the TensorFlow library. You will build a simple version of a Spanish-to-English translator, which will accept a sentence in Spanish and output its English equivalent.

Chapter 5, *Building Your Personal Assistant*, will then look on the practical side of RNNs and have you build a conversational chatbot. This chapter reveals a full implementation of a chatbot system that manages to construct a short conversation. You will then create an end-to-end model that aims to yield meaningful results. You will make use of a high-level TensorFlow-based library called TensorLayer.

Chapter 6, *Improving Your RNN's Performance*, will go through some techniques for improving your RNN. This chapter will focus on improving your RNN's performance with data and tuning. You will also look into optimizing the TensorFlow library for better results.

To get the most out of this book

You need a basic knowledge of Python 3.6.x and basic knowledge of Linux commands. Previous experience with TensorFlow would be helpful, but is not mandatory.

Download the example code files

You can download the example code files for this book from your account at www.packt.com. If you purchased this book elsewhere, you can visit www.packt.com/support and register to have the files emailed directly to you.

You can download the code files by following these steps:

1. Log in or register at www.packt.com.
2. Select the **SUPPORT** tab.
3. Click on **Code Downloads & Errata**.
4. Enter the name of the book in the **Search** box and follow the onscreen instructions.

Once the file is downloaded, please make sure that you unzip or extract the folder using the latest version of:

- WinRAR/7-Zip for Windows
- Zipeg/iZip/UnRarX for Mac
- 7-Zip/PeaZip for Linux

The code bundle for the book is also hosted on GitHub at `https://github.com/PacktPublishing/Recurrent-Neural-Networks-with-Python-Quick-Start-Guide`. In case there's an update to the code, it will be updated on the existing GitHub repository.

We also have other code bundles from our rich catalog of books and videos available at `https://github.com/PacktPublishing/`. Check them out!

Download the color images

We also provide a PDF file that has color images of the screenshots/diagrams used in this book. You can download it here: `https://www.packtpub.com/sites/default/files/downloads/9781789132335_ColorImages.pdf`.

Conventions used

There are a number of text conventions used throughout this book.

`CodeInText`: Indicates code words in text, database table names, folder names, filenames, file extensions, pathnames, dummy URLs, user input, and Twitter handles. Here is an example: "Mount the downloaded `WebStorm-10*.dmg` disk image file as another disk in your system."

A block of code is set as follows:

```
def generate_data():
    inputs = input_values()
    return inputs, output_values(inputs)
```

When we wish to draw your attention to a particular part of a code block, the relevant lines or items are set in bold:

```
loss = tf.nn.softmax_cross_entropy_with_logits_v2(labels=Y,
    logits=prediction)
total_loss = tf.reduce_mean(loss)
```

Any command-line input or output is written as follows:

```
import tensorflow as tf
import random
```

Bold: Indicates a new term, an important word, or words that you see onscreen. For example, words in menus or dialog boxes appear in the text like this. Here is an example: "Select **System info** from the **Administration** panel."

Warnings or important notes appear like this.

Tips and tricks appear like this.

Get in touch

Feedback from our readers is always welcome.

General feedback: If you have questions about any aspect of this book, mention the book title in the subject of your message and email us at customercare@packtpub.com.

Errata: Although we have taken every care to ensure the accuracy of our content, mistakes do happen. If you have found a mistake in this book, we would be grateful if you would report this to us. Please visit www.packt.com/submit-errata, selecting your book, clicking on the Errata Submission Form link, and entering the details.

Piracy: If you come across any illegal copies of our works in any form on the Internet, we would be grateful if you would provide us with the location address or website name. Please contact us at copyright@packt.com with a link to the material.

If you are interested in becoming an author: If there is a topic that you have expertise in and you are interested in either writing or contributing to a book, please visit authors.packtpub.com.

Reviews

Please leave a review. Once you have read and used this book, why not leave a review on the site that you purchased it from? Potential readers can then see and use your unbiased opinion to make purchase decisions, we at Packt can understand what you think about our products, and our authors can see your feedback on their book. Thank you!

For more information about Packt, please visit `packt.com`.

Introducing Recurrent Neural Networks

1

This chapter will introduce you to the theoretical side of the **recurrent neural network (RNN)** model. Gaining knowledge about what lies behind this powerful architecture will give you a head start on mastering the practical examples that are provided later in the book. Since you may often find yourself in a situation where a critical decision for your application is needed, it is essential to be aware of the building parts of this model. This will help you act appropriately for the situation.

The prerequisite knowledge for this chapter includes basic linear algebra (matrix operations). A basic knowledge in deep learning and neural networks is also a plus. If you are new to that field, I would recommend first watching the great series of videos made by Andrew Ng (https://www.youtube.com/playlist?list=PLkDaE6sCZn6Ec-XTbcX1uRg2_u4xOEky0); they will help you make your first steps so you are prepared to expand your knowledge. After reading the chapter, you will be able to answer questions such as the following:

- What is an RNN?
- Why is an RNN better than other solutions?
- How do you train an RNN?
- What are some problems with the RNN model?

What is an RNN?

An RNN is one powerful model from the deep learning family that has shown incredible results in the last five years. It aims to make predictions on sequential data by utilizing a powerful memory-based architecture.

But how is it different from a standard neural network? A normal (also called **feedforward**) neural network acts like a mapping function, where a single input is associated with a single output. In this architecture, no two inputs share knowledge and the each moves in only one direction—starting from the input nodes, passing through hidden nodes, and finishing at the output nodes. Here is an illustration of the aforementioned model:

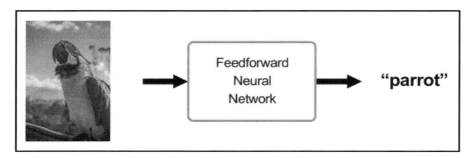

On the contrary, a recurrent (also called feedback) neural network uses an additional memory state. When an input A_1 (word **I**) is added, the network produces an output B_1 (word **love**) and stores information about the input A_1 in the memory state. When the next input A_2 (word **love**) is added, the network produces the associated output B_2 (word **to**) with the help of the memory state. Then, the memory state is updated using information from the new input A_2. This operation is repeated for each input:

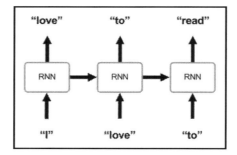

You can see how with this method our predictions depend not only on the current input, but also on previous data. This is the reason why RNNs are the state-of-the-art model for dealing with sequences. Let's illustrate this with some examples.

A typical use case for the feedforward architecture is image recognition. We can see its application in agriculture for analyzing plants, in healthcare for diagnosing diseases, and in driverless cars for detecting pedestrians. Since no output in any of these examples requires specific information from a previous input, the feedforward network is a great fit for such problems.

There is also another set of problems, which are based on sequential data. In these cases, predicting the next element in the sequence depends on all the previous elements. The following is a list of several examples:

- Translating text to speech
- Predicting the next word in a sentence
- Converting audio to text
- Language translation
- Captioning videos

RNNs were first introduced in the 1980s with the invention of the Hopfield network. Later, in 1997, Hochreiter and Schmidhuber proposed an advanced RNN model called **long short-term memory (LSTM)**. It aims to solve some major issues with the simplest recurrent neural network model, which we will reveal later in the chapter. A more recent improvement to the RNN family was presented in 2014 by Chung et al. This new architecture, called Gated Recurrent Unit, solves the same problem as LSTM but in a simpler manner.

In the next chapters of this book, we will go over the aforementioned models and see how they work and why researchers and large companies are using them on a daily basis to solve fundamental problems.

Comparing recurrent neural networks with similar models

In recent years, RNNs, similarly to any neural network model, have become widely popular due to the easier access to large amounts of structured data and increases in computational power. But researchers have been solving sequence-based problems for decades with the help of other methods, such as the Hidden Markov Model. We will briefly compare this technique to an RNNs and outline the benefits of both approaches.

The **Hidden Markov Model (HMM)** is a probabilistic sequence model that aims to assign a label (class) to each element in a sequence. HMM computes the probability for each possible sequence and picks the most likely one.

Both the HMM and RNN are powerful models that yield phenomenal results but, depending on the use case and resources available, RNN can be much more effective.

Hidden Markov model

The following are the pros and cons of a Hidden Markov Model when solving sequence-related tasks:

- **Pros:** Less complex to implement, works faster and as efficiently as RNNs on problems of medium difficulty.
- **Cons:** HMM becomes exponentially expensive with the desire to increase accuracy. For example, predicting the next word in a sentence may depend on a word from far behind. HMM needs to perform some costly operations to obtain this information. That is the reason why this model is not ideal for complex tasks that require large amounts of data.

 These costly operations include calculating the probability for each possible element with respect to all the previous elements in the sequence.

Recurrent neural network

The following are the pros and cons of a recurrent neural network when solving sequence-related tasks:

- **Pros**: Performs significantly better and is less expensive when working on complex tasks with large amounts of data.
- **Cons**: Complex to build the right architecture suitable for a specific problem. Does not yield better results if the prepared data is relatively small.

As a result of our observations, we can state that RNNs are slowly replacing HMMs in the majority of real-life applications. One ought to be aware of both models, but with the right architecture and data, RNNs often end up being the better choice.

Nevertheless, if you are interested in learning more about hidden Markov models, I strongly recommend going through some video series (https://www.youtube.com/watch?v=TPRoLreU91A) and papers of example applications, such as *Introduction to Hidden Markov Models* by Degirmenci (Harvard University) (https://scholar.harvard.edu/files/adegirmenci/files/hmm_adegirmenci_2014.pdf) or *Issues and Limitations of HMM in Speech Processing: A Survey* (https://pdfs.semanticscholar.org/8463/dfee2b46fa813069029149e8e80cec95659f.pdf).

Understanding how recurrent neural networks work

With the use of a memory state, the RNN architecture perfectly addresses every sequence-based problem. In this section of the chapter, we will go over a full explanation of how this works. You will obtain knowledge about the general characteristics of a neural network as well as what makes RNNs special. This section emphasizes on the theoretical side (including mathematical equations), but I can assure you that once you grasp the fundamentals, any practical example will go smoothly.

To make the explanations understandable, let's discuss the task of generating text and, in particular, producing a new chapter based on one of my favorite book series, *The Hunger Games*, by Suzanne Collins.

Basic neural network overview

At the highest level, a neural network, which solves supervised problems, works as follows:

1. Obtain training data (such as images for image recognition or sentences for generating text)
2. Encode the data (neural networks work with numbers so a numeric representation of the data is required)
3. Build the architecture of your neural network model
4. Train the model until you are satisfied with the results
5. Evaluate your model by making a fresh new prediction

Let's see how these steps are applied for an RNN.

Obtaining data

For the problem of generating a new book chapter based on the book series *The Hunger Games*, you can extract the text from all books in *The Hunger Games* series (*The Hunger Games, Mockingjay,* and *Catching Fire*) by copying and pasting it. To do that, you need to find the books, content online.

Encoding the data

We use *word embeddings* (`https://www.analyticsvidhya.com/blog/2017/06/word-embeddings-count-word2veec/`) for this purpose. Word embedding is a collective name of all techniques where words or phrases from a vocabulary are mapped to vectors of real numbers. Some methods include *one-hot encoding*, *word2vec*, and *GloVe*. You will learn more about them in the forthcoming chapters.

Building the architecture

Each neural network consists of three sets of layers—input, hidden, and output. There is always one input and one output layer. If the neural network is deep, it has multiple hidden layers:

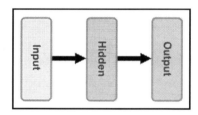

The difference between an RNN and the standard feedforward network comes in the cyclical hidden states. As seen in the following diagram, recurrent neural networks use cyclical hidden states. This way, data propagates from one time step to another, making each one of these steps dependent on the previous:

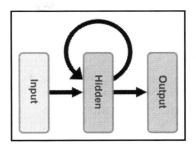

A common practice is to unfold the preceding diagram for better and more fluent understanding. After rotating the illustration vertically and adding some notations and labels, based on the example we picked earlier (generating a new chapter based on *The Hunger Games* books), we end up with the following diagram:

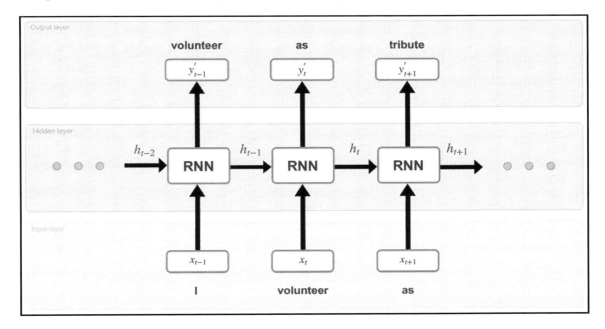

This is an unfolded RNN with one hidden layer. The identically looking sets of (input + hidden RNN unit + output) are actually the different time steps (or cycles) in the RNN. For example, the combination of x_{t-1} + RNN + y'_{t-1} illustrates what is happening at time step $t-1$. At each time step, these operations perform as follows:

1. The network encodes the word at the current time step (for example, *t-1*) using any of the word embedding techniques and produces a vector x_{t-1} (The produced vector can be x_t or x_{t+1} depending on the specific time step)

2. Then, x_{t-1}, the encoded version of the input word **I** at time step *t-1*, is plugged into the RNN cell (located in the hidden layer). After several equations (not displayed here but happening inside the RNN cell), the cell produces an output y'_{t-1} and a memory state h_{t-1}. The memory state is the result of the input x_{t-1} and the previous value of that memory state h_{t-2}. For the initial time step, one can assume that h_0 is a zero vector

3. Producing the actual word (volunteer) at time step *t-1* happens after decoding the output y'_{t-1} using a *text corpus* specified at the beginning of the training

4. Finally, the network moves multiple time steps forward until reaching the final step where it predicts the word

You can see how each one of $\{..., h_{t-1}, h_t, h_{t-1}, ...\}$ holds information about all the previous inputs. This makes RNNs very special and really good at predicting the next unit in a sequence. Let's now see what mathematical equations sit behind the preceding operations.

Text corpus—an array of all words in the example vocabulary.

Training the model

All the magic in this model lies behind the RNN cells. In our simple example, each cell presents the same equations, just with a different set of variables. A detailed version of a single cell looks like this:

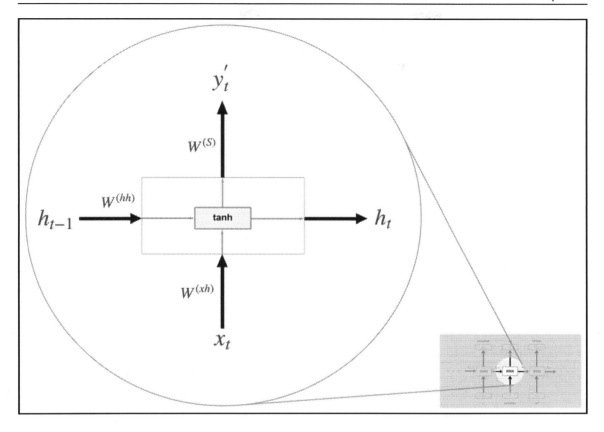

First, let's explain the new terms that appear in the preceding diagram:

- **Weights** ($W^{(xh)}$, $W^{(hh)}$, $W^{(S)}$): A weight is a matrix (or a number) that represents the strength of the value it is applied to. For example, $W^{(xh)}$ determines how much of the input x_t should be considered in the following equations.
If $W^{(xh)}$ consists of high values, then x_t should have significant influence on the end result. The weight values are often initialized randomly or with a distribution (such as normal/Gaussian distribution). It is important to be noted that $W^{(xh)}$, $W^{(hh)}$, and $W^{(S)}$ are the same for each step. Using the backpropagation algorithm, they are being modified with the aim of producing accurate predictions

- **Biases** (b^h, b^s): An offset vector (different for each layer), which adds a change to the value of the output y_t'
- **Activation function (tanh)**: This determines the final value of the current memory state h_t and the output y_t'. Basically, the activation functions map the resultant values of several equations similar to the following ones into a desired range: (-1, 1) if we are using the **tanh** function, (0, 1) if we are using sigmoid function, and (0, +infinity) if we are using ReLu (https://ai. stackexchange.com/questions/5493/what-is-the-purpose-of-an-activation- function-in-neural-networks)

Now, let's go over the process of computing the variables. To calculate h_t and y_t', we can do the following:

$$h_t = tanh(W^{(hh)} * h_{t-1} + W^{(hx)} * x_t + b^h)$$

$$y_t' = softmax(W^{(S)} * h_t + b^S)$$

As you can see, the memory state h_t is a result of the previous value h_{t-1} and the input x_t. Using this formula helps in retaining information about all the previous states.

The input x_t is a one-hot representation of the word *volunteer*. Recall from before that one-hot encoding is a type of word embedding. If the text corpus consists of 20,000 unique words and volunteer is the 19th word, then x_t is a 20,000-dimensional vector where all elements are 0 except the one at the 19th position, which has a value of 1, which suggests that we only taking into account this particular word.

The sum between h_{t-1}, x_t, and b^h is passed to the *tanh* activation function, which squashes the result between -1 and 1 using the following formula:

$$tanh(z) = \frac{e^z - e^{-z}}{e^z + e^{-z}}$$

In this, e = 2.71828 (Euler's number) and z is any real number.

The output y_t' at time step t is calculated using h_t and the `softmax` function. This function can be categorized as an activation with the exception that its primary usage is at the output layer when a probability distribution is needed. For example, predicting the correct outcome in a classification problem can be achieved by picking the highest probable value from a vector where all the elements sum up to 1. Softmax produces this vector, as follows:

$$softmax(z)_i = \frac{e^{z_i}}{e^{z_1} + e^{z_2} + \cdots + e^{z_K}}$$

In this, `e = 2.71828` (Euler's number) and z is a K-dimensional vector. The formula calculates probability for the value at the ith position in the vector z.

After applying the `softmax` function, y_t' becomes a vector of the same dimension as x_t (the corpus size `20,000`) with all its elements having a total sum of 1. With that in mind, finding the predicted word from the text corpus becomes straightforward.

Evaluating the model

Once an assumption for the next word in the sequence is made, we need to assess how good this prediction is. To do that, we need to compare the predicted word y_t' with the actual word from the training data (let's call it y_t). This operation can be accomplished using a loss (cost) function. These types of functions aim to find the error between predicted and actual values. Our choice will be the cross-entropy loss function, which looks like this:

$$J(y, y') = -\sum y_i * log(y_i')$$

Since we are not going to give a detailed explanation of this formula, you can treat it as a black box. If you are curious about how it works, I recommend reading the article *Improving the way neural networks work* by Michael Nielson (`http://neuralnetworksanddeeplearning.com/chap3.html#introducing_the_cross-entropy_cost_function`). A useful thing to know is that the cross-entropy function performs really well on classification problems.

After computing the error, we came to one of the most complex and, at the same time, powerful techniques in deep learning, called backpropagation.

In simple terms, we can state that the backpropagation algorithm traverses backward through all (or several) time steps while updating the weights and biases of the network. After repeating this procedure, and a certain amount of training steps, the network learns the correct parameters and will be able to yield better predictions.

 To clear out any confusion, training and time steps are completely different terms. In one time step, we get a single element from the sequence and predict the next one. A training step is composed of multiple time steps where the number of time steps depends on how large the sequence for this training step is. In addition, time steps are only used in RNNs, but training ones are a general neural network concept.

After each training step, we can see that the value from the loss function decreases. Once it crosses a certain threshold, we can state that the network has successfully learned to predict new words in the text.

The last step is to generate the new chapter. This can happen by choosing a random word as a start (such as: games) and then predicting the next words using the preceding formulas with the pre-trained weights and biases. Finally, we should end up with somewhat meaningful text.

Key problems with the standard recurrent neural network model

Hopefully, now you have a good understanding of how a recurrent neural network works. Unfortunately, this simple model fails to make good predictions on longer and complex sequences. The reason behind this lies in the so-called vanishing/exploding gradient problem that prevents the network from learning efficiently.

As you already know, the training process updates the weights and biases using the backpropagation algorithm. Let's dive one step further into the mathematical explanations. In order to know how much to adjust the parameters (weights and biases), the network computes the derivative of the loss function (at each time step) with respect to the current value of these parameters. When this operation is done for multiple time steps with the same set of parameters, the value of the derivative can become too large or too small. Since we use it to update the parameters, a large value can result in undefined weights and biases and a small value can result in no significant update, and thus no *learning*.

Derivative is a way to show the rate of change; that is, the amount by which a function is changing at one given point. In our case, this is the rate of change of the loss function with respect to the given weights and biases.

This issue was first addressed by Bengio et al. in 1994, which led to an introduction of the LSTM network with the aim of solving the vanishing/exploding gradient problem. Later in the book, we will reveal how LSTM does this in an excellent fashion. Another model, which also overcomes this challenge, is the gated recurrent unit. In Chapter 3, *Generating Your Own Book Chapter,* you will see how this is being done.

For more information on the vanishing/exploding gradient problem, it would be useful to go over Lecture 8 from the course *Natural Language Processing with Deep Learning* by Stanford University (https://www. youtube.com/watch?v=Keqep_PKrY8) and the paper *On the difficulty of training recurrent neural networks* (http://proceedings.mlr.press/v28/pascanu13.pdf).

Summary

In this chapter, we introduce the recurrent neural network model using theoretical explanations together with a particular example. The aim is to grasp the fundamentals of this powerful system so you can understand the programming exercises better. Overall, the chapter included the following:

- A brief introduction to RNNs
- The difference between RNNs and other popular models
- Illustrating the use of RNNs through an example
- The main problems with a standard RNN

In the next chapter, we will go over our first practical exercise using recurrent neural networks. You will get to know the popular TensorFlow library, which makes it easy to build machine learning models. The next section will give you a nice first hands-on experience and prepare you for solving more difficult problems.

External links

- Andrew Ng's deep learning course: `https://www.youtube.com/playlist?list=PLkDaE6sCZn6Ec-XTbcX1uRg2_u4xOEky0`
- Hidden Markov model: `https://www.youtube.com/watch?v=TPRoLreU91A`
- *Introduction to Hidden Markov Models* by Degirmenci: `https://scholar.harvard.edu/files/adegirmenci/files/hmm_adegirmenci_2014.pdf`
- *Issues and Limitations of HMM in Speech Processing: A Survey:* `https://pdfs.semanticscholar.org/8463/dfee2b46fa813069029149e8e80cec95659f.pdf`
- Words embeddings: `https://www.analyticsvidhya.com/blog/2017/06/word-embeddings-count-word2veec/` and `https://towardsdatascience.com/word-embeddings-exploration-explanation-and-exploitation-with-code-in-python-5dac99d5d795`
- *Understanding activation functions:* `https://ai.stackexchange.com/questions/5493/what-is-the-purpose-of-an-activation-function-in-neural-networks`
- *Improving the way neural networks work* by Michael Nielson: `http://neuralnetworksanddeeplearning.com/chap3.html#introducing_the_cross-entropy_cost_function`
- Lecture 8 from the course, *Natural Language Processing with Deep Learning* by Stanford University: `https://www.youtube.com/watch?v=Keqep_PKrY8`
- *On the difficulty of training recurrent neural networks:* `http://proceedings.mlr.press/v28/pascanu13.pdf`

2
Building Your First RNN with TensorFlow

In this chapter, you will gain a hands-on experience of building a **recurrent neural network (RNN)**. First, you will be introduced to the most widely used machine learning library—TensorFlow. From learning the basics to advancing into some fundamental techniques, you will obtain a reasonable understanding of how to apply this powerful library to your applications. Then, you will take on a fairly simple task of building an actual model. The process will show you how to prepare your data, train the network, and make predictions.

In summary, the topics of this chapter include the following:

- **What are you going to build?**: Introduction of your task
- **Introduction to TensorFlow**: Taking first steps into learning the TensorFlow framework
- **Coding the RNN**: You will go through the process of writing your first neural network using TensorFlow. This includes all steps required for a finished solution

The prerequisites for this chapter are basic Python programming knowledge and decent understanding of recurrent neural networks captured in the Chapter 1, *Introducing Recurrent Neural Networks*. After reading this chapter, you should have a full understanding of how to use TensorFlow with Python and how easy and straightforward it is to build a neural network.

What are you going to build?

Your first steps into the practical world of recurrent neural networks will be to build a simple model which determines the parity (http://mathworld.wolfram.com/Parity.html) of a bit sequence . This is a warm-up exercise released by OpenAI in January 2018 (https://blog.openai.com/requests-for-research-2/). The task can be explained as follows:

Given a binary string of a length of 50, determine whether there is an even or odd number of ones. If that number is even, output 0, otherwise 1.

Later in this chapter, we will give a detailed explanation of the solution, together with addressing the difficult parts and how to tackle them.

Introduction to TensorFlow

TensorFlow is an open source library built by Google, which aims to assist developers in creating machine learning models of any kind. The recent improvements in the deep learning space created the need for an easy and fast way of building neural networks. TensorFlow addresses this problem in an excellent fashion, by providing a wide range of APIs and tools to help developers focus on their specific problem, rather than dealing with mathematical equations and scalability issues.

TensorFlow offers two main ways of programming a model:

- Graph-based execution
- Eager execution

Graph-based execution

Graph-based execution is an alternative way of representing mathematical equations and functions. Considering the expression $a = (b*c) + (d*e)$, we can use a graph representation as follows:

1. Separate the expression into the following:
   - $x = b*c$
   - $y = d*e$
   - $a = x+y$

2. Build the following graph:

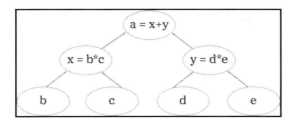

As you can see from the previous example, using graphs lets compute two equations in parallel. This way, the code can be distributed among multiple CPUs/GPUs.

More complex variants of that example are used in TensorFlow for training heavy models. Following that technique, TensorFlow graph-based execution requires a two-step approach when building your neural network. One should first construct the graph architecture and then execute it to receive results.

This approach makes your application run faster and it will be distributed across multiple CPUs, GPUs, and so on. Unfortunately, some complexity comes along with it. Understanding how this way of programming work, and the inability to debug your code in the already familiar way (for example, printing values at any point in your program) makes the graph-based execution (see for more details `http://smahesh.com/blog/2017/07/10/understanding-tensorflow-graph/`) a bit challenging for beginners.

Even though this technique may introduce a new way of programming, our examples will be based upon it. The reason behind this decision lies in the fact that there are many more resources out there and almost every TensorFlow example you come across is graph-based. In addition, I believe it is of vital importance to understand the fundamentals, even if they introduce unfamiliar techniques.

Eager execution

Eager execution is an approach, recently introduced by Google, which, as stated in the documentation (`https://www.tensorflow.org/guide/eager`), uses the following:

An imperative programming environment that evaluates operations immediately, without building graphs: operations return concrete values instead of constructing a computational graph to run later. This makes it easy to get started with TensorFlow and debug models, and it reduces boilerplate as well.

As you can see, there is no overhead to learning the new programming technique and debugging is seamless. For a better understanding, I recommend checking this tutorial from the TensorFlow Conference 2018 (`https://www.youtube.com/watch?v=T8AW0fKP0Hs`).

I must state that, once you learn how to manipulate the TF API, building models becomes really easy on both graph-based and eager execution. Don't panic if the former seems complicated at first—I can assure you that it is worth investing the time to understand it properly.

Coding the recurrent neural network

As mentioned before, the aim of our task is to build a recurrent neural network that predicts the parity of a bit sequence. We will approach this problem in a slightly different way. Since the parity of a sequence depends on the number of ones, we will sum up the elements of the sequence and find whether the result is even or not. If it is even, we will output 0, otherwise, 1.

This section of the chapter includes code samples and goes through the following steps:

- Generating data to train the model
- Building the TensorFlow graph (using TensorFlow's built-in functions for recurrent neural networks)
- Training the neural network with the generated data
- Evaluating the model and determining its accuracy

Generating data

Let's revisit the OpenAI's task (`https://blog.openai.com/requests-for-research-2/`). As stated there, we need to generate a dataset of random 100,000 binary strings of length 50. In other words, our training set will be formed of 100,000 examples and the recurrent neural network will accept 50 time steps. The result of the last time step would be counted as the model prediction.

The task of determining the sum of a sequence can be viewed as a classification problem where the result can be any of the classes from 0 to 50. A standard practice in machine learning is to encode the data into an easily decodable numeric way. But why is that? Most machine learning algorithms cannot accept anything apart from numeric data, so we need to always encode our input/output. This means that, our predictions will also come out in an encoding format. Thus, it is vital to understand the actual value behind these predictions. This means that we need to be able to easily decode them into a human understandable format. A popular way of encoding data for classification problems is one-hot encoding.

Here is an example of that technique.

Imagine the predicted output for a specific sequence is 30. We can encode this number by introducing a 1x50 array where all numbers, except the one in the 30th position, are 0s – [0, 0,..., 0, 1, 0, ..., 0, 0, 0].

Before preparing the actual data, we need to import all of the necessary libraries. To do that, follow this link (https://www.python.org/downloads/) to install Python on your machine. In your command-line/Terminal window install the following packages:

```
pip3 install tensorflow
```

After you have done that, create a new file called ch2_task.py and import the following libraries:

```
import tensorflow as tf
import random
```

Preparing the data requires an input and output value. The input value is a three-dimensional array of a size of [100000, 50, 1], with 100000 items, each one containing 50 one-element arrays (either 0 or 1), and is shown in the following example:

```
[ [ [1], [0], [1], [1], ..., [0], [1] ]
[ [0], [1], [0], [1], ..., [0], [1] ]
[ [1], [1], [1], [0], ..., [0], [0] ]
[ [1], [0], [0], [0], ..., [1], [1] ] ]
```

The following example shows the implementation:

```
num_examples = 100000
num_classes = 50

def input_values():
    multiple_values = [map(int, '{0:050b}'.format(i)) for i in
range(2**20)]
    random.shuffle(multiple_values)
```

```
final_values = []
for value in multiple_values[:num_examples]:
    temp = []
    for number in value:
        temp.append([number])
    final_values.append(temp)
return final_values
```

Here, `num_classes` is the number of time steps in our RNN (50, in this example). The preceding code returns a list with the 100000 binary sequences. The style is not very Pythonic but, written in this way, it makes it easy to follow and understand.

First, we start with initializing the `multiple_values` variable. It contains a binary representation of the first 2^{20} = 1,048,576 numbers, where each binary number is padded with zeros to accommodate the length of 50. Obtaining so many examples minimizes the chance of similarity between any two of them. We use the `map` function together with `int` in order to convert the produced string into a number.

Here is a quick example of how this works. We want to represent the number 2 inside the `multiple_values` array. The binary version of 2 is `'10'`, so the string produced after `'{0:050b}'.format(i)` where `i` = 2, is `'00000000000000000000000000000000000000000000000010'` (48 zeros at the front to accommodate a length of 50). Finally, the `map` function makes the previous string into a number without removing the zeros at the front.

Then, we shuffle the `multiple_values` array, assuring difference between neighboring elements. This is important during backpropagation when the network is trained, because we are iteratively looping throughout the array and training the network at each step using a single example. Having similar values next to each other inside the array may produce biased results and incorrect future predictions.

Finally, we enter a loop, which traverses over all of the binary elements and builds an array similar to the one we saw previously. An important thing to note is the usage of `num_examples`, which slices the array, so we pick only the first 100,000 values.

The second part of this section shows how to generate the expected output (the sum of all the elements in each list from the input set). These outputs are used to evaluate the model and tune the `weight/biases` during backpropagation. The following example shows the implementation:

```
def output_values(inputs):
    final_values = []
    for value in inputs:
        output_values = [0 for _ in range(num_classes)]
```

```
            count = 0
            for i in value:
                count += i[0]
            if count < num_classes:
                output_values[count] = 1
            final_values.append(output_values)
        return final_values
```

The `inputs` parameter is a result of `input_values()` that we declared earlier. The `output_values()` function returns a list of one-hot encoded representations of each member in `inputs`. If the sum of all of the elements in the `[[0], [1], [1], [1], [0], ..., [0], [1]]` sequence is `48`, then its corresponding value inside `output_values` is `[0, 0, 0, ..., 1, 0, 0]` where 1 is at position 48.

Finally, we use the `generate_data()` function to obtain the final values for the network's input and output, as shown in the following example:

```
def generate_data():
    inputs = input_values()
    return inputs, output_values(inputs)
```

We use the previous function to create these two new variables: `input_values`, and `output_values = generate_data()`. One thing to pay attention to is the dimensions of these lists:

- `input_values` is of a size of `[num_examples, num_classes, 1]`
- `output_values` is of a size of `[num_examples, num_classes]`

Where `num_examples = 100000` and `num_classes = 50`.

Building the TensorFlow graph

Constructing the TensorFlow graph is probably the most complex part of building a neural network. We will precisely examine all of the steps so you can obtain a full understanding.

The TensorFlow graph can be viewed as a direct implementation of the recurrent neural network model, including all equations and algorithms introduced in `Chapter 1`, *Introducing Recurrent Neural Networks*.

First, we start with setting the parameters of the model, as shown in the following example:

```
X = tf.placeholder(tf.float32, shape=[None, num_classes, 1])
Y = tf.placeholder(tf.float32, shape=[None, num_classes])
num_hidden_units = 24
weights = tf.Variable(tf.truncated_normal([num_hidden_units, num_classes]))
biases = tf.Variable(tf.truncated_normal([num_classes]))
```

`X` and `Y` are declared as `tf.placeholder`, which inserts a placeholder (inside the graph) for a tensor that will be always fed. Placeholders are used for variables that expect data when training the network. They often hold values for the training input and expected output of the network. You might be surprised why one of the dimensions is `None`. The reason is that we have trained the network using batches. These are collections of several elements from our training data stacked together. When specifying the dimension as None, we let the tensor decide this dimension, calculating it using the other two values.

According to the TensorFlow documentation: A tensor is a generalization of vectors and matrices to potentially higher dimensions. Internally, TensorFlow represents tensors as n-dimensional arrays of base datatypes.

When performing training using batches, we split the training data into several smaller arrays of size—`batch_size`. Then, instead of training the network with all examples at once, we use one batch at a time.

The advantages of this are less memory is required and faster learning is achieved.

The `weight` and `biases` are declared as `tf.Variable`, which holds a certain value during training. This value can be modified. When a variable is first introduced, one should specify an initial value, type, and shape. The type and shape remain constant and cannot be changed.

Next, let's build the RNN cell. If you recall from Chapter 1, *Introducing Recurrent Neural Networks*, an input at time step, *t*, is plugged into an RNN cell to produce an output, y_t, and a hidden state, h_t. Then, the hidden state and the new input at time step (t+1) are plugged into a new RNN cell (which shares the same weights and biases as the previous). It produces its own output, y_{t+1}, and hidden state, h_{t+1}. This pattern is repeated for every time step.

With TensorFlow, the previous operation is just a single line:

```
rnn_cell = tf.contrib.rnn.BasicRNNCell(num_units=num_hidden_units)
```

As you already know, each cell requires an activation function that is applied to the hidden state. By default, TensorFlow chooses **tanh** (perfect for our use case) but you can specify any that you wish. Just add an additional parameter called `activation`.

Both in `weights` and in `rnn_cell`, you can see a parameter called `num_hidden_units`. As stated here (`https://stackoverflow.com/questions/37901047/what-is-num-units-in-tensorflow-basiclstmcell`), the `num_hidden_units` is a direct representation of the learning capacity of a neural network. It determines the dimensionality of both the memory state, h_t, and the output, y_t.

The next step is to produce the output of the network. This can also be implemented with a single line:

```
outputs, state = tf.nn.dynamic_rnn(rnn_cell, inputs=X,
dtype=tf.float32)
```

Since X is a batch of input sequences, then `outputs` represents a batch of outputs at every time step in all sequences. To evaluate the prediction, we need the value of the last time step for every output in the batch. This happens in three steps, explained in the following bulleted examples:

- We get the values from the last time step: `outputs = tf.transpose(outputs, [1, 0, 2])`

This would reshape the output's tensor from (1000, 50, 24) to (50, 1,000, 24) so that the outputs from the last time step in every sequence are accessible to be gathered using the following: `last_output = tf.gather(outputs, int(outputs.get_shape()[0]) - 1)`.

Let's review the following diagram to understand how this `last_output` is obtained:

The previous diagram shows how one input example of 50 steps is plugged into the network. This operation should be done 1,000 times for each individual example having 50 steps but, for the sake of simplicity, we are showing only one example.

After iteratively going through each time step, we produce 50 outputs, each one having the dimensions (24, 1). So, for one example of 50 input time steps, we produce 50 output steps. Presenting all of the outputs mathematically results in a (1,000, 50, 24) matrix. The height of the matrix is 1,000—the number of individual examples. The width of the matrix is 50—the number of time steps for each example. The depth of the matrix is 24—the dimension of each element.

To make a prediction, we only care about `output_last` at each example, and since the number of examples is 1,000, we only need 1,000 output values. As seen in the previous example, we transpose the matrix (1000, 50, 24) into (50, 1000, 24), which will make it easier to get `output_last` from each example. Then, we use `tf.gather` to obtain the `last_output` tensor which has size of (1000, 24, 1).

Final lines of building our graph include:

- We predict the output of the particular sequence:

```
prediction = tf.matmul(last_output, weights) + biases
```

Using the newly obtained tensor, `last_output`, we can calculate a prediction using the weights and biases.

- We evaluate the output based on the expected value:

```
loss = tf.nn.softmax_cross_entropy_with_logits_v2(labels=Y,
logits=prediction)
total_loss = tf.reduce_mean(loss)
```

We can use the popular cross entropy loss function in a combination with `softmax`. If you recall from `Chapter 1`, *Introducing Recurrent Neural Networks*, the `softmax` function transforms a tensor to emphasize the largest values and suppress values that are significantly below the maximum value. This is done by normalizing the values from the initial array to ones that add up to 1. For example, the input `[0.1, 0.2, 0.3, 0.4, 0.1, 0.2, 0.3]` becomes `[0.125, 0.138, 0.153, 0.169, 0.125, 0.138, 0.153]`. The cross entropy is a loss function that computes the difference between the `label` (expected values) and `logits` (predicted values).

Since `tf.nn.softmax_cross_entropy_with_logits_v2` returns a 1-D tensor of a length of `batch_size` (declared below), we use `tf.reduce_mean` to compute the mean of all elements in that tensor.

As a final step, we will see how TensorFlow makes it easy for us to optimize the weights and biases. Once we have obtained the loss function, we need to perform a backpropagation algorithm, adjusting the weights and biases to minimize the loss. This can be done in the following way:

```
learning_rate = 0.001
optimizer =
tf.train.AdamOptimizer(learning_rate=learning_rate).minimize(loss=total_los
s)
```

learning_rate is one of the model's hyperparameters and is used when optimizing the loss function. Tuning this value is essential for better performance, so feel free to adjust it and evaluate the results.

Minimizing the error of the loss function is done using an Adam optimizer. Here (https://stats.stackexchange.com/questions/184448/difference-between-gradientdescentoptimizer-and-adamoptimizer-tensorflow) is a good explanation of why it is preferred over the Gradient descent.

We have just built the architecture of our recurrent neural network. Let's put everything together, as shown in the following example:

```
X = tf.placeholder(tf.float32, shape=[None, num_classes, 1])
Y = tf.placeholder(tf.float32, shape=[None, num_classes])

num_hidden_units = 24

weights = tf.Variable(tf.truncated_normal([num_hidden_units, num_classes]))
biases = tf.Variable(tf.truncated_normal([num_classes]))

rnn_cell = tf.contrib.rnn.BasicRNNCell(num_units=num_hidden_units,
activation=tf.nn.relu)
outputs1, state = tf.nn.dynamic_rnn(rnn_cell, inputs=X, dtype=tf.float32)
outputs = tf.transpose(outputs1, [1, 0, 2])

last_output = tf.gather(outputs, int(outputs.get_shape()[0]) - 1)
prediction = tf.matmul(last_output, weights) + biases

loss = tf.nn.softmax_cross_entropy_with_logits_v2(labels=Y,
logits=prediction)
total_loss = tf.reduce_mean(loss)

learning_rate = 0.001
optimizer =
tf.train.AdamOptimizer(learning_rate=learning_rate).minimize(loss=total_los
s)
```

The next task is to train the neural network using the TensorFlow graph in combination with the previously generated data.

Training the RNN

In this section, we will go through the second part of a TensorFlow program—executing the graph with a predefined data. For this to happen, we will use the Session object, which encapsulates an environment in which the tensor objects are executed.

The code for our training is shown in the following example:

```
batch_size = 1000
number_of_batches = int(num_examples/batch_size)
epoch = 100
with tf.Session() as sess:
    sess.run(tf.global_variables_initializer())
    X_train, y_train = generate_data()
    for epoch in range(epoch):
        iter = 0
        for _ in range(number_of_batches):
            training_x = X_train[iter:iter+batch_size]
            training_y = y_train[iter:iter+batch_size]
            iter += batch_size
            _, current_total_loss = sess.run([optimizer, total_loss],
            feed_dict={X: training_x, Y: training_y})
            print("Epoch:", epoch, "Iteration:", iter, "Loss",
current_total_loss)
            print("_____")
```

First, we initialize the batch size. At each training step, the network is tuned, based on examples from the chosen batch. Then, we compute the number of batches as well as the number of epochs—this determines how many times our model should loop through the training set. `tf.Session()` encapsulates the code in a TensorFlow `Session` and `sess.run(tf.global_variables_initializer())` (https://stackoverflow.com/ questions/44433438/understanding-tf-global-variables-initializer) makes sure all variables hold their values.

Then, we store an individual batch from the training set in `training_x` and `training_y`.

The last, and most, important part of training the network comes with the usage of `sess.run()`. By calling this function, you can compute the value of any tensor. In addition, one can specify as many arguments as you want by ordering them in a list—in our case, we have specified the optimizer and loss function. Remember how, while building the graph, we created placeholders for holding the values of the current batch? These values should be mentioned in the `feed_dict` parameter when running `Session`.

Training this network can take around four or five hours. You can verify that it is learning by examining the value of the loss function. If its value decreases, then the network is successfully modifying the weights and biases. If the value is not decreasing, you most likely need to make some additional changes to optimize the performance. These will be explained in `Chapter 6`, *Improving Your RNN Performance*.

Evaluating the predictions

Testing the model using a fresh new example can be accomplished in the following way:

```
prediction_result = sess.run(prediction, {X: test_example})
largest_number_index = prediction_result[0].argsort()[-1:][::-1]

print("Predicted sum: ", largest_number_index, "Actual sum:", 30)
print("The predicted sequence parity is ", largest_number_index % 2, " and
it should be: ", 0)
```

This is where `test_example` is an array of a size of `(1 x num_classes x 1)`.

Let `test_example` be as follows:

```
[[[1],[0],[0],[1],[1],[0],[1],[1],[1],[0],[1],[0],[0],[1],[1],[0],[1],[1],[
1],[0],
[1],[0],[0],[1],[1],[0],[1],[1],[1],[0],[1],[0],[0],[1],[1],[0],[1],[1],[1]
,[0],
[1],[0],[0],[1],[1],[0],[1],[1],[1],[0]]]
```

The sum of all elements in the above array is equal to 30. With the last line, `prediction_result[0].argsort()[-1:][::-1]`, we can find the index of the largest number. The index would tell us the sum of the sequence. As a last step, we need to find the remainder when this number is divided by 2. This will give us the parity of the sequence.

Both training and evaluation are done together after you run `python3 ch2_task.py`. If you want to only do evaluation, comment out the lines between 70 and 91 from the program and run it again.

Summary

In this chapter, you explored how to build a simple recurrent neural network to solve the problem of identifying sequence parity. You obtained a brief understanding of the TensorFlow library and how it can be utilized for building deep learning models. I hope the study of this chapter leaves you more confident in your deep learning knowledge, as well as excited to learn and grow more in this field.

In the next chapter, you will go a step further by implementing a more sophisticated neural network for the task of generating text. You will gain both theoretical and practical experience. This will result in you learning about a new type of network, GRU, and understanding how to implement it in TensorFlow. In addition, you will face the challenge of formatting your input text correctly as well as using it for training the TensorFlow graph.

I can assure you that an exciting learning experience is coming, so I cannot wait for you to be part of it.

External links

- Parity: http://mathworld.wolfram.com/Parity.html
- Request for Research 2.0 by OpenAI: https://blog.openai.com/requests-for-research-2/
- Eager execution documentation: https://www.tensorflow.org/guide/eager
- Eager execution (TensorFlow Conference 2018): https://www.youtube.com/watch?v=T8AW0fKP0Hs
- Python installation: https://www.python.org/downloads/
- Understanding num_hidden_units : https://stackoverflow.com/questions/37901047/what-is-num-units-in-tensorflow-basiclstmcell
- Adam versus Gradient descent optimizer: https://stats.stackexchange.com/questions/184448/difference-between-gradientdescentoptimizer-and-adamoptimizer-tensorflow
- Understanding sess.run(tf.global_variables_initializer(): https://stackoverflow.com/questions/44433438/understanding-tf-global-variables-initializer

3

Generating Your Own Book Chapter

In this chapter, we will take a step further into exploring the TensorFlow library and how it can be leveraged to solve complex tasks. In particular, you will build a neural network that generates a new (non-existing) chapter of a book by learning patterns from the existing chapters. In addition, you will grasp more of the TensorFlow functionalities, such as saving/restoring a model, and so on.

This chapter will also introduce a new and more powerful recurrent neural network model called the **gated recurrent unit (GRU)**. You will learn how it works and why we are choosing it over the simple RNN.

In summary, the topics of the chapter include the following:

- Why use the GRU network? You will learn how the GRU network works, what problems it solves, and what its benefits are.
- Generating your book chapter—you will go step by step over the process of generating a book chapter. This includes collecting and formatting the training data, building the TensorFlow graph of the GRU model, training the network and, finally, generating the text word by word.

By the end of the chapter, you should have gained both a theoretical and a practical knowledge that will give you the freedom to experiment with any problems of medium difficulty.

Why use the GRU network?

In recent years, the recurrent neural network model has presented fascinating results which can even be seen in real-life applications like language translation, speech synthesis and more. A phenomenal application of GRUs happens to be text generation. With the current state-of-the-art models, we can see results which, a decade ago, were just a dream. If you want to truly appreciate these results, I strongly recommend you read Andrej Karpathy's article on *The Unreasonable Effectiveness of Recurrent Neural Networks* (http://karpathy. github.io/2015/05/21/rnn-effectiveness/).

Having said that, we can introduce the **Gated Recurrent Unit (GRU)** as a model which sits behind these exceptional outcomes. Another model of that kind is the **Long Short-Term Memory (LSTM)** which is slightly more advanced. Both architectures aim to solve the vanishing gradient problem—a major issue with the simple RNN model. If you recall from Chapter 1, *Introducing Recurrent Neural Networks*, the problem represents the network's inability to learn long-distance dependencies and, thus, it cannot make accurate predictions on complex tasks.

Both the GRU and LSTM deal with that problem using, so-called, gates. These gates decide what information to erase or propagate towards the prediction.

We will first focus on the GRU model since it is simpler and easier to understand and, then, you will have the chance to explore the LSTM model in the upcoming chapters.

As mentioned above, the GRU's main objective is to yield excellent results on long sequences. It achieves this by modifying the standard RNN cell with the introduction of update and reset gates. This network works the same way as a normal RNN model in terms of inputs, memory states and outputs. The key difference lies in the specifics of the cell at each time step. You will understand that better by using the following graph:

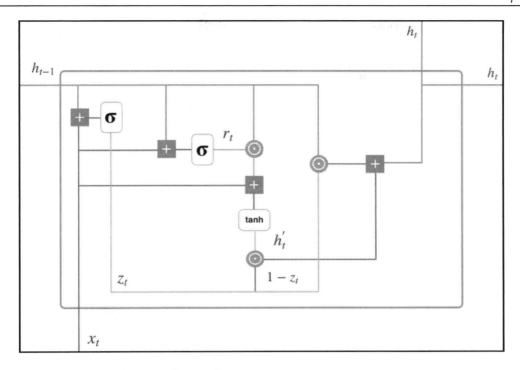

These are the notations for the preceding graph:

| "plus" operation | "sigmoid" function | "Hadamard product" operation | "tanh" function |

The illustration presents a single GRU cell. The cell accepts x_t and h_{t-1} as inputs where x_t is a vector representation of the input word at time step, t and h_{t-1} is the memory state from the previous step $t-1$. Furthermore, the cell outputs the calculated memory state of the current step t. If you recall from before, the aim of this intermediate memory state is to pass information through all time steps and keep or discard knowledge. The preceding process should already be familiar to you from the RNN explanation in Chapter 1, *Introducing Recurrent Neural Networks*.

The new and interesting thing is what happens inside this GRU cell. The calculations aim to decide what information from x_t and h_{t-1} should be passed forward or eliminated. That decision-making process is handled by the following set of equations:

$$z_t = \sigma(W^{(z)} x_t + U^{(z)} h_{t-1})$$

$$r_t = \sigma(W^{(r)} x_t + U^{(r)} h_{t-1})$$

$$h'_t = tanh(W x_t + r_t \odot U h_{t-1})$$

$$h_t = z_t \odot h_{t-1} + (1 - z_t) \odot h'_t$$

- The first equation presents the update gate. Its purpose is to determine how much of the past information should be propagated in the future. To do that, first we multiple the input x_t with its own weight $W^{(z)}$ and then sum the result with the other multiplication between the memory state from the last step h_{t-1} and its weight $U^{(z)}$. The exact values of these weights are determined during training. This is shown in the following screenshot:

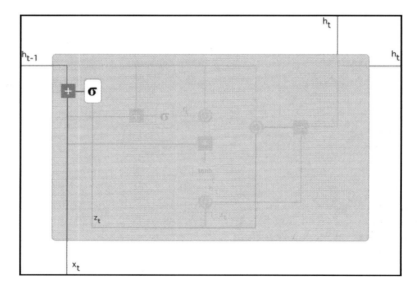

- The second equation presents the reset gate. As the name states, this gate is used to decide how much of the past information should be omitted. Again, using x_t and h_{t-1} we calculate its value. The difference is that instead of using the same weights, our network learns a different set of weights—$W^{(r)}$ and $U^{(r)}$. This is shown in the following screenshot:

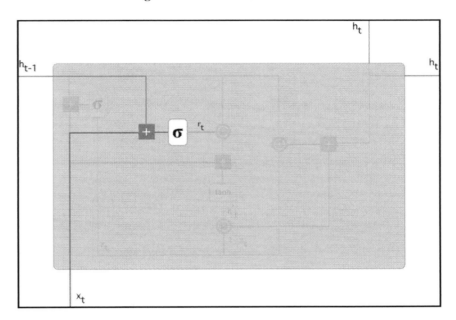

Both the update and reset gate us the sigmoid as a final step when producing the value. If you recall from Chapter 1, *Introducing Recurrent Neural Networks*, the sigmoid (https://www.youtube.com/watch?v=WcDtwxi7Ickt=3s) is a type of activation function which squashes the input between 0 and 1:

- The third equation is a temporary internal memory state which uses the input x_t and the reset gate r_t to store the relevant information from the past. Here we use a *tanh* activation function which is similar to a sigmoid, but instead squashes the output between −1 and 1. Here (https://stats.stackexchange.com/questions/101560/tanh-activation-function-vs-sigmoid-activation-function) is a good explanation of the difference between both activations. As you can see, we use a different notation ⊙ called element-wise or Hadamard multiplication (https://www.youtube.com/watch?v=2GPZ1RVhQWY).

If you have the vectors [1, 2, 3] and [0, -1, 4] the Hadamard product will be [1*0, 2*(-1), 3*4] = [0, -2, 12]. This is shown in the following screenshot:

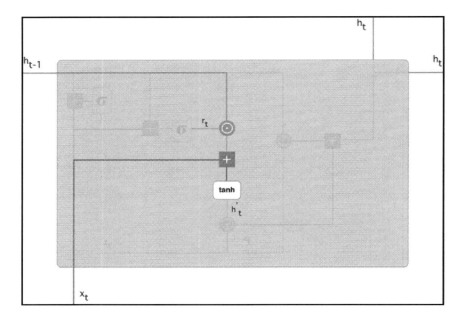

- The final equation calculates memory state h_t at the current time step t. To do this, we use the temporary internal memory state $h_t^{'}$, the previous memory state h_{t-1} and the update gate z_t. Again, we are using the element-wise multiplication which makes the update gate decide how much information to propagate forward. Let's illustrate this with an example:

Imagine you want to do sentiment analysis on a book review to determine how people feel about a certain book. Let's say that the review starts like this: *The book was super exciting and I liked it a lot. It reveals the story of a young woman....* Here we want to keep the first part of the review until the end, so that we make an accurate prediction. In that case, the network will learn to make z_t close to 1, so that $1 - z_t$ is close to 0. This way all future memory states will hold mostly information about this first part (*The book was super exciting and I liked it a lot.*) and won't take into account any irrelevant information that comes next.

Combining the above equations results in a powerful model, which can learn to keep full or partial information at any step, and enhance the final prediction. You can easily see how this solution solves the vanishing gradient problem by letting the network (based on the weights) decide what should influence the predictions.

Generating your book chapter

After going through the theoretical part of this chapter, we are ready to dive into coding. I hope you grasp the fundamental behind the GRU model and will feel comfortable seeing the notations in the TensorFlow program. It consists of five parts, most of which may be familiar to you from Chapter 2, *Building Your First RNN with TensorFlow*:

- **Obtaining the book text**: this one is really straightforward. Your task is to assure a lot of plain text is ready for training.
- **Encoding the text**: this one can be challenging, since we need to accommodate the encoding with the proper dimensions. Sometimes, this operation can take more time than expected but it is a requirement for compiling the program flawlessly. There are different types of encoding algorithms and we will choose a fairly simple one so you fully understand its true essence.
- **Building the TensorFlow graph**: this operation should be familiar to you from Chapter 2, *Building Your First RNN with TensorFlow*. We will use similar steps with the difference that now the operational cell is a GRU instead of a normal RNN.
- **Training the network**: this step should also be familiar to you from Chapter 2, *Building Your First RNN with TensorFlow*. We will again use batches to make our training faster and occupy less memory.
- **Generating your new text**: this is the new and unique step in our program. We will use the already trained weights and biases to predict the sequences of words. Using appropriate hyperparameters with a large set of data can yield understandable paragraphs which one can easily assume are real.

You will be writing the code in a new file called ch3_task.py. First, install the Python libraries using the following code:

```
pip3 install tensorflow
pip3 install numpy
```

Then, open ch3_task.py and import the preceding libraries, as shown in the following code:

```
import numpy as np
import tensorflow as tf
import sys
import collections
```

Now it is time to explore the steps.

Obtaining the book text

The first step in building any machine learning task is to obtain the data. In a professional environment you would divide it into training, validation and testing data. Normally the distribution is 60%, 20%, 20% People often confuse validation with test data or even omit using the former. The validation data is used to evaluate the model while tuning the hyperparameters. In contrast, the test data is used only to give an overall evaluation of the model. You SHOULD NOT use the test data to make changes on your model. Since the task is to generate text, our data will be used only for training. Then, we can leverage the model to guess words one by one.

Our aim is to yield a meaningful new chapter based on the *The Hunger Games* books. We should store the text in a new file called the_hunger_games.txt.

First, we need to build our dictionary using that file. This will happen using the two functions called get_words(file_name) and build_dictionary(words) as shown in the following example:

```
def get_words(file_name):
    with open(file_name) as file:
        all_lines = file.readlines()
    lines_without_spaces = [x.strip() for x in all_lines]
    words = []
    for line in lines_without_spaces:
        words.extend(line.split())
    words = np.array(words)
    return words
```

The previous function aims to create a list of all the words in the_hunger_games.txt. Now let's build the actual dictionary using the following code:

```
def build_dictionary(words):
    most_common_words = collections.Counter(words).most_common()
    word2id = dict((word, id) for (id, (word, _)) in
```

```
enumerate(most_common_words))
    id2word = dict((id, word) for (id, (word, _)) in
enumerate(most_common_words))
    return most_common_words, word2id, id2word
```

Here we use the Python built-in library collections. It can easily create a list of tuples where each tuple is formed of a string (word) and time of occurrences of this word in the list words. Thus, `most_common_words` does not contain any duplicate elements.

The dictionaries `word2id` and `id2word` associate a number with each word which ensures a straightforward access to all words.

Finally, we execute the `get_words()` and `build_dictionary()` functions, so that the words and dictionaries can be accessed globally, as shown in the following example:

```
words = get_words("the_hunger_games.txt")
most_common_words, word2id, id2word = build_dictionary(words)
most_common_words_length = len(most_common_words)
```

Encoding the text

This part shows how to encode our dataset using the popular one-hot encoding. The reason behind this operation lies in the fact that any neural network operates using some sort of numerical representation of strings.

First, we declare `section_length = 20` which represents the length of a single section in our encoded dataset. This dataset is a collection of sections where each section has 20 one-hot encoded words.

Then, we store the sections of 20 words in the `input_values` array. The 21st word is used as the output value for that particular section. This means that, during training, the network learns that the words *I love reading non-fiction...I can find these type of* (example sequence of 20 words extracted from the training set) are followed by *book*.

After that, comes the one-hot encoding which is also quite straightforward. We create two arrays of zeros with dimensions (`num_sections`, `section_length`, `most_common_words_length`)—for the inputs and (`num_sections`, `most_common_words_length`)—for the outputs. We iterate over the `input_values` and find the index of each word in each section. Using these indices, we replace the values in the one-hot arrays with `1`.

The code for this is in the following example:

```
section_length = 20

def input_output_values(words):
    input_values = []
    output_values = []
    num_sections = 0
    for i in range(len(words) - section_length):
        input_values.append(words[i: i + section_length])
        output_values.append(words[i + section_length])
        num_sections += 1

    one_hot_inputs = np.zeros((num_sections, section_length,
most_common_words_length))
    one_hot_outputs = np.zeros((num_sections, most_common_words_length))

    for s_index, section in enumerate(input_values):
        for w_index, word in enumerate(section):
            one_hot_inputs[s_index, w_index, word2id[word]] = 1.0
        one_hot_outputs[s_index, word2id[output_values[s_index]]] = 1.0

    return one_hot_inputs, one_hot_outputs
```

Finally, we store the encoded words in two global variables (we also use the parameter words from the previous part of that chapter), as shown in the following example:

```
training_X, training_y = input_output_values(words)
```

Building the TensorFlow graph

This step builds the most fundamental part of our program—the neural network graph.

First, we start by initializing the hyperparameters of the model, as shown in the following example:

```
learning_rate = 0.001
batch_size = 512
number_of_iterations = 100000
number_hidden_units = 1024
```

One often experiments with the above values until the model receives decent results:

- The `learning_rate` (https://towardsdatascience.com/understanding-learning-rates-and-how-it-improves-performance-in-deep-learning-d0d4059c1c10) is used in backpropagation and should have a fairly small value.

- The `batch_size` determines how many elements each batch should have. The data is often divided into batches so that training is faster and requires less memory. You will see more about the usage of batches later.

- `number_of_iterations` is how many training steps we should take. A training step includes picking one batch from the data and performing forward and then backward propagation, which updates the weights and biases.

- `number_hidden_units` (https://stackoverflow.com/questions/37901047/what-is-num-units-in-tensorflow-basiclstmcell) is the number of units used in any RNN cell. There is actually a pretty neat formula (https://stats.stackexchange.com/questions/181/how-to-choose-the-number-of-hidden-layers-and-nodes-in-a-feedforward-neural-network) which calculates that number based on the input and output neurons of the network.

After we have defined the above parameters, it is time to specify our graph. This is demonstrated in the following snippets of code:

- We start with the TensorFlow placeholder X which holds the training data at that current batch, and Y—which holds the predicted data at that current batch. This is shown in the following code:

```
X = tf.placeholder(tf.float32, shape=[batch_size, section_length,
most_common_words_length])
y = tf.placeholder(tf.float32, shape=[batch_size,
most_common_words_length])
```

- Then, we initialize our weights and biases using a normal distribution. The dimensions of weights is `[number_hidden_units, most_common_words_length]` which assures correct multiplication in our prediction. The same logic goes for biases with dimensions `[most_common_words_length]`. This is shown in the following example:

```
weights = tf.Variable(tf.truncated_normal([num_hidden_units,
most_common_words_length]))
biases =
tf.Variable(tf.truncated_normal([most_common_words_length]))
```

- Next, we specify the GRU cell. All the complex logic learned in the first section of that chapter is hidden behind the previous line of code. Chapter 2, *Building Your First RNN with TensorFlow,* explained why we then pass the parameter num_units, which is shown in the following example:

```
gru_cell = tf.contrib.rnn.GRUCell(num_units=num_hidden_units)
```

- Then, we calculate the outputs using the GRU cell and the inputs X. An important step is to transpose those outputs with [1, 0, 2] permutations.

```
outputs, state = tf.nn.dynamic_rnn(gru_cell, inputs=X,
 dtype=tf.float32)
outputs = tf.transpose(outputs, perm=[1, 0, 2])

last_output = tf.gather(outputs, int(outputs.get_shape()[0]) - 1)
```

Let's review the following illustration to understand how this last_output is obtained:

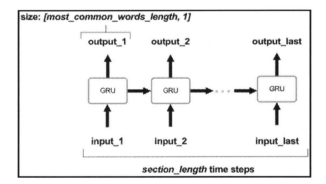

The illustration shows how one input example of section_length steps is plugged into the network. This operation should be done batch_size times for each individual example having section_length steps, but, for the sake of simplicity, we are showing only one example.

After iteratively going through each time step, we produce a section_length number of outputs, each one having the dimensions [most_common_words_length, 1]. So, for one example of the section_length input time steps, we produce section_length output steps. Presenting all outputs mathematically results in a [batch_size, section_length, most_common_words_length] matrix. The height of the matrix is batch_size - the number of individual examples in a single batch. The width of the matrix is section_length - the number of time steps for each example. The depth of the matrix is most_common_words_length - the dimension of each element.

To make a prediction, we are only concerned about the `output_last` at each example and, since the number of examples is `batch_size`, we only need the `batch_size` output values. As seen previously, we reshape the matrix [`batch_size, section_length, most_common_words_length`] into [`section_length, batch_size, most_common_words_length`] which will make it easier to get the `output_last` from each example. Then, we use `tf.gather` to obtain the `last_output` tensor.

Below is a code implementation of the above explanation:

- As we now have the array with these final step values, we can make our prediction and use it (in a combination with the label values as seen on the fourth line of the previous example) to find the loss at this training step. Since the loss has the same dimensions as the labels (expected output values) and logits (predicted output values), we use `tf.reduce_mean` to produce a single `total_loss`. This is demonstrated in the following code:

```
prediction = tf.matmul(last_output, weights) + biases

loss = tf.nn.softmax_cross_entropy_with_logits_v2(labels=y,
logits=prediction)
total_loss = tf.reduce_mean(loss)
```

- Finally, the `total_loss` is used during backpropagation, with the aim of improving the model's performance by adjusting its weights and biases. This is done through `tf.train.AdamOptimizer` which is run during training, and that is detailed in the following section:

```
optimizer =
tf.train.AdamOptimizer(learning_rate=learning_rate).minimize(
loss=total_loss)
```

Training the network

Once the model is built, we need to train it using the pre-collected data. This operation follows the code snippets below:

- We start by initializing all the TensorFlow variables. Then, we have the `iter_offset` which makes sure the right batch is extracted from the data. This is shown in the following code:

```
with tf.Session() as sess:
    sess.run(tf.global_variables_initializer())
    iter_offset = 0
```

- Next, the `tf.train.Saver()` creates a saver object which periodically saves the model locally. This helps us in case something happens and our training is interrupted. Also, it helps us during the prediction phase to look up the pre-trained parameters and so we do not have to run the training every time we want to make a prediction:

```
saver = tf.train.Saver()
```

Now, comes the time for the actual training. We loop through the training data while calculating the optimizer using the individual batches. These calculations will minimize the loss function and we can see it decreasing by printing its value, as shown in the snippets as follows:

- First, we need to divide the data into batches. This is done with the help of the `iter_offset` parameter. It keeps track of the lower bound of each batch so we always get the next batch from the training set, as shown in the following code:

```
for iter in range(number_of_iterations):
    length_X = len(training_X)

    if length_X != 0:
        iter_offset = iter_offset % length_X
    if iter_offset <= length_X - batch_size:
        training_X_batch = training_X[iter_offset: iter_offset +
          batch_size]
        training_y_batch = training_y[iter_offset: iter_offset +
          batch_size]
        iter_offset += batch_size
    else:
        add_from_the_beginning = batch_size - (length_X -
          iter_offset)
        training_X_batch =
          np.concatenate((training_X[iter_offset: length_X], X[0:
          add_from_the_beginning]))
        training_y_batch =
          np.concatenate((training_y[iter_offset:
          length_X], y[0: add_from_the_beginning]))
        iter_offset = add_from_the_beginning
```

- Next, we should perform the training by calculating the `optimizer` and `total_loss`. We can run a TensorFlow session with the current batch input and output. Finally, we should print the loss function, so we can keep track of our progress. If our network is training successfully, the value of the loss function should decrease at each step:

```
_, training_loss = sess.run([optimizer, total_loss], feed_dict=
 {X: training_X_batch, y: training_y_batch})
if iter % 10 == 0:
    print("Loss:", training_loss)
    saver.save(sess, 'ckpt/model', global_step=iter)
```

Normally, this training takes several hours to finish. You can speed up the process by increasing your computational power. We will discuss some techniques to do that in `Chapter 6`, *Improve Your RNN Performance*.

Generating your new text

After you have successfully trained your model, it is time to generate your new *The Hunger Games* chapter.

The preceding code can be divided into two parts:

- Training the model using a custom input
- Predicting the next 1,000 words in the sequence

Let's explore the code snippets below:

- In the beginning, we initialized a custom input of 21 words (we used the (`section_length + 1`) in order to match the model's dimensions). This input is used to give a starting point on our prediction. Next, we will train the existing network with it, so that the weight and biases are optimized for the upcoming predictions, as shown in the following example:

```
starting_sentence = 'I plan to make the world a better place
 because I love seeing how people grow and do in their lives '
```

- Then, we can restore the saved model from the `ckpt` folder in order to train it using the newest input, as demonstrated in the following code:

```
with tf.Session() as sess:
    sess.run(tf.global_variables_initializer())
    model = tf.train.latest_checkpoint('ckpt')
    saver = tf.train.Saver()
    saver.restore(sess, model)
```

- We should then encode that input in a one-hot vector with dimensions `[1,` `section_length,` `most_common_words_length]`. That array should be fed into our model so that the predicted words follow the sequence. You may notice that we omit the last word and add it later on to produce the `text_next_X` array (see the following code). We do that in order to give an unbiased head start to our text generation. This is demonstrated in the following example:

```
generated_text = starting_sentence
words_in_starting_sentence = starting_sentence.split()
test_X = np.zeros((1, section_length,
most_common_words_length))

for index, word in enumerate(words_in_starting_sentence[:-1]):
    if index < section_length:
        test_X[0, index, word2id[word]] = 1
```

- Finally, we should train the network using the encoded input sentence. To maintain an unbiased head start of the training, we need to add the last word from the sentence before starting the prediction shown in the following example. A slightly confusing part can be the `np.concatenate` method. We should first reshape the `text_X` to easily append the last section and then reshape the result to accommodate the prediction evaluation. This is shown in the following example:

```
_ = sess.run(prediction, feed_dict={X: test_X})
test_last_X = np.zeros((1, 1, most_common_words_length))
test_last_X[0, 0, word2id[words_in_starting_sentence[-1]]] = 1
test_next_X = np.reshape(np.concatenate((test_X[0, 1:],
test_last_X[0])), (1, section_length, most_common_words_length)
```

- The last part is actually generating the words. At each step (of 1,000 steps) we can calculate the prediction using the current `test_next_X`. Then, we can remove the first character from the current `test_next_X` and append the prediction. This way we constantly keep a set of 20 words where the last element is a fresh new prediction. This is shown in the following example:

```
for i in range(1000):
    test_prediction = prediction.eval({X: test_next_X})[0]
    next_word_one_hot = prediction_to_one_hot(test_prediction)
    next_word = id2word[np.argmax(next_word_one_hot)]
    generated_text += next_word + " "
    test_next_X =
      np.reshape(np.concatenate((test_next_X[0,1:],
                      np.reshape(next_word_one_hot, (1,
                      most_common_words_length)))),
```

```
                    (1, section_length,
                    most_common_words_length))
        print("Generated text: ", generated_text)
```

The method `prediction_to_one_hot` encodes the prediction into a one hot encoding array. This is defined in the following example:

```
def prediction_to_one_hot(prediction):
    zero_array = np.zeros(np.shape(prediction))
    zero_array[np.argmax(prediction)] = 1
    return zero_array
```

After running the code, you should see the final chapter printed out in the console. If there is inconsistency among the words, you need to tweak some of the hyperparameters. I will explain in the last chapter how you can optimize your model and receive good performance. Train a network with the snippets above and keep me updated about your performance. I would be really happy to see your end results.

Summary

In this chapter, you went through the process of building a book chapter generator using a Gated Recurrent Unit neural network. You understood what sits behind this powerful model and how you can put it into practice with a handful of lines of code using TensorFlow. In addition, you faced the challenge of preparing and clearing your data so that your model is trained correctly.

In the next chapter, you will fortify your skills by implementing your first real-life practical application—a language translator. You have probably faced the online Google Translate software and were amazed by how well it worked. In the next chapter, you will understand what sits behind a sophisticated system like that and why its level of accuracy has increased drastically in recent years.

I hope the current chapter advanced your deep learning knowledge and that you are excited to be exploring more from the world of recurrent neural networks. I cannot wait for you to start the next section.

External links

- The Unreasonable Effectiveness of Recurrent Neural Networks—http://karpathy.github.io/2015/05/21/rnn-effectiveness/
- Sigmoid activation function—https://www.youtube.com/watch?v=WcDtwxi7Ick t=3s
- The difference between sigmoid and tanh activation function—https://stats.stackexchange.com/questions/101560/tanh-activation-function-vs-sigmoid-activation-function
- Element-wise multiplication—https://www.youtube.com/watch?v=2GPZlRVhQWY
- Learning rate in the neural network—https://towardsdatascience.com/understanding-learning-rates-and-how-it-improves-performance-in-deep-learning-d0d4059c1c10
- The number of hidden units in TensorFlow—https://stackoverflow.com/questions/37901047/what-is-num-units-in-tensorflow-basiclstmcell
- The formula for calculating the number of hidden units—https://stats.stackexchange.com/questions/181/how-to-choose-the-number-of-hidden-layers-and-nodes-in-a-feedforward-neural-network

4

Creating a Spanish-to-English Translator

This chapter will push your neural network knowledge even further by introducing state-of-the-art concepts at the core of today's most powerful language translation systems. You will build a simple version of a Spanish-to-English translator, which accepts a sentence in Spanish and outputs its English equivalent.

This chapter includes the following sections:

- **Understanding the translation model**: This section is entirely focused on the theory behind this system.
- **What an LSTM network is**: We'll be understanding what sits behind this advanced version of recurrent neural networks.
- **Understanding sequence-to-sequence network with attention**: You will grasp the theory behind this powerful model, get to know what it actually does, and why it is so widely used for different problems.
- **Building the Spanish-to-English translator**: This section is entirely focused on implementing the knowledge acquired up to this point in a working program. It includes the following:
    - Training the model
    - Predicting English translations
    - Evaluating the accuracy of the model

Understanding the translation model

Machine translation is often done using so-called **statistical machine translation**, based on statistical models. This approach works very well, but a key issue is that, for every pair of languages, we need to rebuild the architecture. Thankfully, in 2014, Cho *et al.* (`https://arxiv.org/pdf/1406.1078.pdf`) came out with a paper that aims to solve this, and other problems, using the increasingly popular recurrent neural networks. The model is called sequence-to-sequence, and has the ability to be trained on any pair of languages by just providing the right amount of data. In addition, its power lies in its ability to match sequences of different lengths, such as in machine translation, where a sentence in English may have a different size when compared to a sentence in Spanish. Let's examine how these tasks are achieved.

First, we will introduce the following diagram and explain what it consists of:

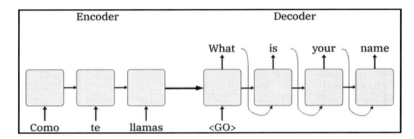

The architecture has three major parts: the **encoder** RNN network (on the left side), the intermediate state (marked by the middle arrow), and the **decoder** RNN network (on the right side). The flow of actions for translating the sentence **Como te llamas?** (Spanish) into **What is your name?** (English) is as follows:

- Encode the Spanish sentence, using the encoder RNN, into the intermediate state
- Using that state and the decoder RNN, generate the output sentence in English

This simple approach works with short and simple sentences, but, in practice, the true use of translation models lies in longer and more complicated sequences. That is why we are going to extend our basic approach using the powerful LSTM network and an attention mechanism. Let's explore these techniques in the following sections.

What is an LSTM network?

LSTM (long short-term memory) network is an advanced RNN network that aims to solve the vanishing gradient problem and yield excellent results on longer sequences. In the previous chapter, we introduced the GRU network, which is a simpler version of LSTM. Both include memory states that determine what information should be propagated further at each timestep. The LSTM cell looks as follows:

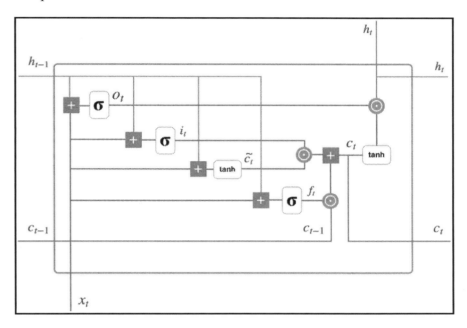

Let's introduce the main equations that will clarify the preceding diagram. They are similar to the ones for gated recurrent units (see Chapter 3, *Generating Your Own Book Chapter*). Here is what happens at every given timestep, *t*:

$$o_t = \sigma(W^{(o)}x_t + U^{(o)}h_{t-1})$$

$$i_t = \sigma(W^{(i)}x_t + U^{(i)}h_{t-1})$$

$$\tilde{c}_t = \tanh(W^{(c)}x_t + U^{(c)}h_{t-1})$$

$$f_t = \sigma(W^{(f)}x_t + U^{(f)}h_{t-1})$$

o_t is the **output gate**, which determines what exactly is important for the current prediction and what information should be kept around for the future. i_t is called the **input gate**, and determines how much we concern ourselves about the current vector (cell). $\tilde{c}_t$ is the value for the new memory cell. f_t is the **forget gate**, which determines how much to forget from the current vector (if the forget gate is 0, we are entirely forgetting the past). All four, $o_t, i_t, \tilde{c}_t, f_t$, have the same equation insight (with its corresponding weights), but $\tilde{c}_t$ uses tanh and the others use sigmoid.

Finally, we have the final memory cell c_t and final hidden state h_t :

$$c_t = f_t \circ c_{t-1} + i_t \circ \tilde{c}_t$$

The final memory cell separates the input and forget gate, and decides how much of the previous output c_{t-1} should be kept and how much of the current output $\tilde{c}_t$ should be propagated forward (in simple terms, this means: *forget the past or not, take the input or not*). The *dot* sign is called the Hadamard product—if x = [1, 2, 3] and y = [4, 5, 6], then x dot y = [1*4, 2*5, 3*6] = [4, 10, 18].

The final hidden state is defined as follows:

$$h_t = o_t \circ tanh(c_t)$$

It decides whether to expose the content of the cell at this particular timestep. Since some of the information c_t from the current cell may be omitted in h_t, we are passing c_t forward to be used in the next timesteps.

This same system is repeated multiple times through the neural network. Often, it is the case that several LSTM cells are stacked together and use shared weights and biases.

Two great sources for enhancing your knowledge on LSTMs are Colah's article *Understanding LSTM Network* (http://colah.github.io/posts/2015-08-Understanding-LSTMs/) and the Stanford University lecture on LSTM (https://www.youtube.com/watch?v=QuELiw8tbx8) by Richard Socher.

Understanding the sequence-to-sequence network with attention

Since you have already understood how the LSTM network works, let's take a step back and look at the full network architecture. As we said before, we are using a sequence-to-sequence model with an attention mechanism. This model consists of LSTM units grouped together, forming the encoder and decoder parts of the network.

In a simple sequence-to-sequence model, we input a sentence of a given length and create a vector that captures all the information in that particular sentence. After that, we use the vector to predict the translation. You can read more about how this works in a wonderful Google paper (https://arxiv.org/pdf/1409.3215.pdf) in the *External links* section at the end of this chapter.

That approach is fine, but, as in every situation, we can and must do better. In that case, a better approach would be to use an attention mechanism. This is motivated by the way a person does language translation. A person doesn't read the input sentence, then hide the text while they try to write down the output sentence. They are continuously keeping track of the original sentence while making the translation. This is how the attention mechanism works. At every timestep of the decoder, the network decides what and how many of the encoder inputs to use. To make that decision, special weights are attached to every encoder word. In practice, the attention mechanism tries to solve a fundamental problem with recurrent neural networks—the ability to remember long-term dependencies.

A good illustration of the attention mechanism can be seen here:

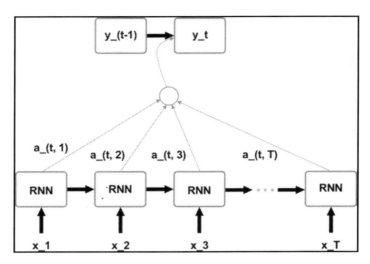

$x_1, x_2, x_3, \ldots, x_t$ are the inputs and $\cdots, y_{t-1}, y_t, \cdots$ are the predicted outputs. You can see the attention weights represented as $a_{t,1}, a_{t,2}, a_{t,3}, \cdots, a_{t,T}$, each one attached to its corresponding input. These weights are learned during training and they decide the influence of a particular input on the final output. This makes every output y_t dependent on a weighted combination of all the input states.

Unfortunately, the attention mechanism comes with a cost. Consider the following, from a WildML article (http://www.wildml.com/2016/01/attention-and-memory-in-deep-learning-and-nlp/):

> *If we look a bit more closely at the equation for attention, we can see that attention comes at a cost. We need to calculate an attention value for each combination of input and output word. If you have a 50-word input sequence and generate a 50-word output sequence, that would be 2500 attention values. That's not too bad, but if you do character-level computations and deal with sequences consisting of hundreds of tokens, the above attention mechanisms can become prohibitively expensive.*

Despite this, the attention mechanism remains a state-of-the-art model for machine translation that produces excellent results. The preceding statement only shows that there is plenty of room for improvement, so we should try to contribute to its development as much as possible.

Building the Spanish-to-English translator

I hope the previous sections left you with a good understanding of the model we are about to build. Now, we are going to get practical and write the code behind our translation system. We should end up with a trained network capable of predicting the English version of any sentence in Spanish. Let's dive into programming.

Preparing the data

The first step, as always, is to collect the needed data and prepare it for training. The more complicated our systems become, the more complex it is to massage the data and reform it into the right shape. We are going to use Spanish-to-English phrases from the OpenSubtitles free data source (`http://opus.nlpl.eu/OpenSubtitles.php`). We will accomplish that task using the `data_utils.py` script, which you can find on the provided GitHub repo (`https://github.com/simonnoff/Recurrent-Neural-Networks-with-Python-Quick-Start-Guide`). There you can also find more details on which datasets to download from OpenSubtitles. The file calculates the following properties, which could be used further in our model:

- `spanish_vocab`: A collection of all words in the Spanish training set, ordered by frequency
- `english_vocab`: A collection of all words in the English training set, ordered by frequency
- `spanish_idx2word`: A dictionary of key and word, where the key is the order of the word in `spanish_vocab`
- `spanish_word2idx`: A reversed version of `spanish_idx2word`
- `english_idx2word`: A dictionary of key and word, where the key is the order of the word in `english_vocab`
- `english_word2idx`: A reversed version of the `english_idx2word`

- x: An array of arrays of numbers. We produce that array by first reading the Spanish text file line by line, and storing these lines of words in separate arrays. Then, we encode each array of a sentence into an array of numbers where each word in the sentence is replaced with its index, based on spanish_word2idx
- Y: An array of arrays of numbers. We produce that array by first reading the English text file line by line and storing these lines of words in separate arrays. Then, we encode each array of a sentence into an array of numbers where each word in the sentence is replaced with its index, based on english_word2idx

You will see, in the following sections, how these collections are used during the training and testing of the model. The next step is to construct the TensorFlow graph.

Constructing the TensorFlow graph

As an initial step, we import the required Python libraries (you can see this in the neural_machine_translation.py file):

```
import tensorflow as tf
import numpy as np
from sklearn.model_selection import train_test_split
import data_utils
import matplotlib.pyplot as plt
```

tensorflow and numpy should already be familiar to you. matplotlib is a handy python library used for visualizing data (you will see how we use it shortly). Then, we use the train_test_split function of sklearn to split the data into random train and test arrays.

We also import data_utils, which is used to access the data collections mentioned in the previous section.

An important modification to do before splitting the data is making sure each of the arrays in *X* and *Y* is padded to indicate the start of a new sequence:

```
def data_padding(x, y, length = 15):
    for i in range(len(X)):
        x[i] = x[i] + (length - len(x[i])) * [spanish_word2idx['<pad>']]
        y[i] = [english_word2idx['<go>']] + y[i] + (length - len(y[i])) *
[english_word2idx['<pad>']]
```

Then, we split the data as follows:

```
X_train,  X_test, Y_train, Y_test = train_test_split(X, Y, test_size = 0.1)
```

Now, it is time to define the actual TensorFlow graph. We start with the variables that determine the input and output sequence length:

```
input_sequence_length = 15
output_sequence_length = 16
```

Then, we calculate the size of each vocabulary:

```
spanish_vocab_size = len(spanish_vocab) + 2 # + <pad>, <unk>
english_vocab_size = len(english_vocab) + 4 # + <pad>, <eos>, <go>
```

The <pad> symbol is used to align the time steps, <go> is used to indicate beginning of decoder sequence, and <eos> indicates empty spaces.

After that, we initialize our TensorFlow placeholders:

```
encoder_inputs = [tf.placeholder(dtype=tf.int32, shape=[None],
name="encoder{}".format(i)) for i in range(input_sequence_length)]

decoder_inputs = [tf.placeholder(dtype=tf.int32, shape=[None],
name="decoder{}".format(i)) for i in range(output_sequence_length)]

targets = [decoder_inputs[i] for i in range(output_sequence_length - 1)]
targets.append(tf.placeholder(dtype = tf.int32, shape=[None],
name="last_output"))

target_weights = [tf.placeholder(dtype = tf.float32, shape = [None],
name="target_w{}".format(i)) for i in range(output_sequence_length)]
```

- encoder_inputs: This holds values for the Spanish training input words.
- decoder_inputs: This holds values for the English training input words.
- target: This holds the real values of the English predictions. It has the same length as the decoder_inputs, where every word is the next predicted.
- target_weights: This is a tensor that gives weights to all predictions.

The final two steps of building the graph are generating the outputs and optimizing the weights and biases of the network.

The former uses the handy TensorFlow function, `tf.contrib.legacy_seq2seq.embedding_attention_seq2seq` (https://www.tensorflow.org/api_docs/python/tf/contrib/legacy_seq2seq/embedding_attention_seq2seq), which builds a sequence-to-sequence network with attention mechanism and returns the generated outputs from the decoder network. The implementation is as follows:

```
size = 512 # num_hidden_units
embedding_size = 100

with tf.variable_scope("model_params"):
    w_t = tf.get_variable('proj_w', [english_vocab_size, size], tf.float32)
    b = tf.get_variable('proj_b', [english_vocab_size], tf.float32)
    w = tf.transpose(w_t)
    output_projection = (w, b)
    outputs, states =
tf.contrib.legacy_seq2seq.embedding_attention_seq2seq(
                    encoder_inputs,
                    decoder_inputs,
                    tf.contrib.rnn.BasicLSTMCell(size),
                    num_encoder_symbols=spanish_vocab_size,
                    num_decoder_symbols=english_vocab_size,
                    embedding_size=embedding_size,
                    feed_previous=False,
                    output_projection=output_projection,
                    dtype=tf.float32)
```

Let's discuss the function's parameters:

- `encoder_inputs` and `decoder_inputs` contain values for each training pair of Spanish and English sentences.
- `tf.contrib.rnn.BasicLSTMCell(size)` is the RNN cell used for the sequence model. This is an LSTM cell with `size` (=512) number of hidden units.
- `num_encoder_symbols` and `num_decoder_symbols` are the Spanish and English dictionaries for the model.
- `embedding_size` represents the length of the embedding vector for each word. This vector can be obtained using the `word2vec` algorithm and helps the network in learning during backpropagation.
- `feed_previous` is a Boolean value that indicates whether or not to use the previous output at a certain timestep as the next decoder input.

- `output_projection` contains a pair of the network's weights and biases. As you can see from the preceding code block, the weights have the `[english_vocab_size, size]` shape and the biases have the `[english_vocab_size]` shape.

After computing the outputs, we need to optimize these weights and biases by minimizing the loss function of that model. For that purpose, we will be using the `tf.contrib.legacy_seq2seq.sequence_loss` TensorFlow function, as follows:

```
loss = tf.contrib.legacy_seq2seq.sequence_loss(outputs, targets,
target_weights, softmax_loss_function = sampled_loss)

learning_rate = 5e-3 (5*10^(-3) = 0.005)
optimizer = tf.train.AdamOptimizer(learning_rate).minimize(loss)
```

We supply the predicted `outputs`, along with the actual values, `targets`, of the network. In addition, we provide a slight modification of the standard softmax loss function.

Finally, we define the optimizer that aims to minimize the loss function.

To clarify the confusion around the `sample_loss` variable, we will give its definition as follows:

```
def sampled_loss(labels, logits):
    return tf.nn.sampled_softmax_loss(
        weights=w_t,
        biases=b,
        labels=tf.reshape(labels, [-1, 1]),
        inputs=logits,
        num_sampled=size,
        num_classes=english_vocab_size
    )
```

This `softmax` function is used only for training. You can learn more about it through the TensorFlow documentation (`https://www.tensorflow.org/api_docs/python/tf/nn/sampled_softmax_loss`).

These equations result in a fully functional TensorFlow graph for our sequence-to-sequence model with attention mechanism. Once again, you may be amazed how little code is required to build a powerful neural network that yields excellent results.

Next, we will plug the data collections into this graph and actually train the model.

Training the model

Training the neural network is accomplished using the same pattern as before:

```
def train():
    init = tf.global_variables_initializer()
    saver = tf.train.Saver()
    with tf.Session() as sess:
        sess.run(init)
        for step in range(steps):
            feed = feed_dictionary_values(X_train, Y_train)
            sess.run(optimizer, feed_dict=feed)
            if step % 5 == 4 or step == 0:
                loss_value = sess.run(loss, feed_dict = feed)
                losses.append(loss_value)
                print("Step {0}/{1} Loss {2}".format(step, steps,
                loss_value))
            if step % 20 == 19:
                saver.save(sess, 'ckpt/', global_step = step)
```

The interesting part from the preceding implementation is the feed_dictionary_values function, which forms the placeholders from the X_train and Y_train:

```
def feed_dictionary_values(x, y, batch_size):
    feed = {}
    indices_x = np.random.choice(len(x), size=batch_size, replace=False)
    indices_y = np.random.choice(len(y), size=batch_size, replace=False)

    for i in range(input_sequence_length):
        feed[encoder_inputs[i].name] = np.array([x[j][i] for j in
indices_x], dtype=np.int32)

    for i in range(output_sequence_length):
        feed[decoder_inputs[i].name] = np.array([y[j][i] for j in
indices_y], dtype=np.int32)

    feed[targets[len(targets)-1].name] = np.full(shape = [batch_size],
fill_value=english_word2idx['<pad>'], dtype=np.int32)

    for i in range(output_sequence_length - 1):
        batch_weights = np.ones(batch_size, dtype=np.float32)
        target = feed[decoder_inputs[i+1].name]
        for j in range(batch_size):
            if target[j] == english_word2idx['<pad>']:
                batch_weigths[j] = 0.0
        feed[target_weights[i].name] = batch_weigths

    feed[target_weights[output_sequence_length - 1].name] =
```

```
np.zeros(batch_size, dtype=np.float32)

    return feed
```

Let's break down the above function line by line.

It needs to return a dictionary with the values of all placeholders. Recall that their names are:

```
"encoder0", "encoder1", ..., "encoder14" (input_sequence_length=15),
"decoder0", "decoder1" through to "decoder15" (output_sequence_length=16),
"last_output", "target_w0", "target_w1", and so on, through to "target_w15"
```

indices_x is an array of 64 (batch_size) randomly selected indices in the range of 0 and len(X_train).

indices_y is an array of 64 (batch_size) randomly selected indices in the range of 0 and len(Y_train).

The "encoder-" values are obtained by finding the array at each index from indices_x and collecting the values for the specific encoder.

Similarly, the "decoder-" values are obtained by finding the array at each index from indices_y and collecting the values for the specific decoder.

Consider the following example: Let's say our X_train is [[x11, x12, ...], [x21, x22, ...], ...], indices_x is [1, 0, ...], then "encoder0" will be [x21, x11, ...] and will contain the 0-th element of all arrays from X_train that have their index stored in indices_x.

The value of last_output is an array of the batch_size size filled only with the number 3 (the associated index of the symbol "<pad>").

Finally, the "target_w-" elements are arrays of 1's and 0's of the batch_size size. These arrays contain 0 at the indices of "<pad>" values from the decoder arrays. Let's illustrate this statement with the example:

If the value of "decoder0" is [10, 8, 3, ...] where 3 is the index of "<pad>" from the en_idx2word array, our "target0" would be [1, 1, 0, ...].

The last "target15" is an array with only 0's.

Having the preceding calculations in mind, we can start training our network. The process will take some time, since we need to iterate over 1,000 steps. Meanwhile, we will be storing the trained parameters at every 20 steps, so we can use them later for prediction.

Predicting the translation

After we have trained the model, we will use its parameters to translate some sentences from Spanish to English. Let's create a new file called predict.py and write our prediction code there. The logic will work as follows:

- Define exactly the same sequence-to-sequence model architecture as used during training
- Use the already trained weights and biases to produce an output
- Encode a set of Spanish sentences, ready for translation
- Predict the final results and print the equivalent English sentences

As you can see, this flow is pretty straightforward:

1. To implement it, we first import two Python libraries together with the neural_machine_translation.py file (used for training):

```
import tensorflow as tf
import numpy as np
import neural_machine_translation as nmt
```

2. Then, we define the model with the associated placeholders:

```
# Placeholders
encoder_inputs = [tf.placeholder(dtype = tf.int32, shape =
[None],
name = 'encoder{}'.format(i)) for i in
range(nmt.input_sequence_length)]
decoder_inputs = [tf.placeholder(dtype = tf.int32, shape =
[None],
name = 'decoder{}'.format(i)) for i in
range(nmt.output_sequence_length)]
with tf.variable_scope("model_params", reuse=True):
    w_t = tf.get_variable('proj_w', [nmt.english_vocab_size,
    nmt.size], tf.float32)
    b = tf.get_variable('proj_b', [nmt.english_vocab_size],
     tf.float32)
    w = tf.transpose(w_t)
```

```
output_projection = (w, b)
outputs, states =
tf.contrib.legacy_seq2seq.embedding_attention_seq2seq(
        encoder_inputs,
        decoder_inputs,
        tf.contrib.rnn.BasicLSTMCell(nmt.size),
        num_encoder_symbols = nmt.spanish_vocab_size,
        num_decoder_symbols = nmt.english_vocab_size,
        embedding_size = nmt.embedding_size,
        feed_previous = True,
        output_projection = output_projection,
        dtype = tf.float32)
```

3. Using the outputs from the TensorFlow function, we calculate the final translations as follows:

```
outputs_proj = [tf.matmul(outputs[i], output_projection[0]) +
output_projection for i in range(nmt.output_sequence_length)]
```

4. The next step is to define the input sentences and encode them using the encoding dictionary:

```
spanish_sentences = ["Como te llamas", "Mi nombre es", "Estoy
   leyendo un libro","Que tal", "Estoy bien", "Hablas espanol",
   "Que hora es", "Hola", "Adios", "Si", "No"]

spanish_sentences_encoded = [[nmt.spanish_word2idx.get(word,
   0) for word in sentence.split()] for sentence in
   spanish_sentences]

for i in range(len(spanish_sentences_encoded)):
    spanish_sentences_encoded[i] += (nmt.input_sequence_length -
    len(spanish_sentences_encoded[i])) *
    [nmt.spanish_word2idx['<pad>']]
```

As you can see, we are also padding the input sentences so they match the length of the placeholder (`nmt.input_sequence_length`).

5. Finally, we will be using `spanish_sentences_encoded` with the preceding TensorFlow model to calculate the value of `outputs_proj` and yield our results:

```
saver = tf.train.Saver()
path = tf.train.latest_checkpoint('ckpt')
with tf.Session() as sess:
    saver.restore(sess, path)

    feed = {}
        for i in range(nmt.input_sequence_length):
```

```
        feed[encoder_inputs[i].name] =
np.array([spanish_sentences_encoded[j][i] for j in
range(len(spanish_sentences_encoded))], dtype = np.int32)

     feed[decoder_inputs[0].name] =
 np.array([nmt.english_word2idx['<go>']] *
len(spanish_sentences_encoded), dtype = np.int32)
    output_sequences = sess.run(outputs_proj, feed_dict = feed)

    for i in range(len(english_sentences_encoded)):
        ouput_seq = [output_sequences[j][i] for j in
          range(nmt.output_sequence_length)]
        words = decode_output(ouput_seq)
      for j in range(len(words)):
        if words[j] not in ['<eos>', '<pad>', '<go>']:
            print(words[j], end=" ")
      print('\n------------------------------')
```

6. Now, we define the `decode_output` function, together with a detailed explanation of its functionality:

```
def decode_output(output_sequence):
    words = []
    for i in range(nmt.output_sequence_length):
        smax = nmt.softmax(output_sequence[i])
        maxId = np.argmax(smax)
      words.append(nmt.english_idx2word[maxId])
    return words
```

7. We prepare the feed dictionary in the same way as using the placeholders' names. For `encoder_inputs`, we use values from `spanish_sentences_encoded`. For `decoder_inputs`, we use the values saved in our model's checkpoint folder.

8. Using the preceding data, our model calculates the `output_sentences`.

9. Finally, we use the `decode_output` function to convert the predicted `output_sentences` matrix into an actual sentence. For that, we use the `english_idx2word` dictionary.

After running the preceding code, you should see the original sentence in Spanish, together with its translation in English. The correct output is as follows:

```
1------------------------------
Como te llamas
What's your name

2------------------------------
```

```
Mi nombre es
My name is

3------------------------------
Estoy leyendo un libro
I am reading a book

4------------------------------
Que tal
How are you

5------------------------------
Estoy bien
I am good

6------------------------------
Hablas espanol
Do you speak Spanish

7------------------------------
Que hora es
What time is it

8------------------------------
Hola
Hi

9------------------------------
Adios
Goodbye

10------------------------------
Si
Yes

11------------------------------
No
No
```

Next, we will see how to evaluate our results and identify how well our translation model has performed.

Evaluating the final results

Translation models are typically evaluated using the so-called BLEU score (https://www.youtube.com/watch?v=DejHQYAGb7Q). This is an automatically generated score that compares a human-generated translation with the prediction. It looks for the presence and absence of particular words, their ordering, and any distortion—that is, how much they are separated in the output.

A BLEU score varies between 0 and 1, where 0 is produced if there are no matching words between the prediction and the human-generated sentence, and 1 when both sentences match perfectly.

Unfortunately, this score can be sensitive about word breaks. If the word breaks are positioned differently, the score may be completely off.

A good machine translation model, such as Google's Multilingual Neural Machine Translation System, achieves score of around 38.0 (0.38*100) on Spanish-to-English translation. This is an example of an exceptionally performing model. The result is pretty remarkable but, as you can see, there is a lot of room for improvement.

Summary

This chapter walked you through building a fairly sophisticated neural network model using the sequence-to-sequence model implemented with the TensorFlow library.

First, you went through the theoretical part, gain an understanding of how the model works under the hood and why its application has resulted in remarkable achievements. In addition, you learned how an LSTM network works and why it is easily considered the best RNN model.

Second, you saw how you can put the knowledge acquired here into practice using just several lines of code. In addition, you gain an understanding of how to prepare your data to fit the sequence-to-sequence model. Finally, you were able to successfully translate Spanish sentences into English.

I really hope this chapter left you more confident in your deep learning knowledge and armed you with new skills that you can apply to future applications.

External links

- Sequence to Sequence model (Cho et al. 2014): `https://arxiv.org/pdf/1406.1078.pdf`
- Understanding LSTM Network: `http://colah.github.io/posts/2015-08-Understanding-LSTMs/`
- Stanford University lecture on LSTM: `https://www.youtube.com/watch?v=QuELiw8tbx8`
- Sequence to sequence learning using Neural Network: `https://arxiv.org/pdf/1409.3215.pdf`
- WildML article on *Attention and Memory in Deep Learning and NLP*: `http://www.wildml.com/2016/01/attention-and-memory-in-deep-learning-and-nlp/`
- OpenSubtitles: `http://opus.nlpl.eu/OpenSubtitles.php`
- `tf.contrib.legacy_seq2seq.embedding_attention_seq2seq`: `https://www.tensorflow.org/api_docs/python/tf/contrib/legacy_seq2seq/embedding_attention_seq2seq`
- `tf.nn.sampled_softmax_loss`: `https://www.tensorflow.org/api_docs/python/tf/nn/sampled_softmax_loss`
- BLEU score: `https://www.youtube.com/watch?v=DejHQYAGb7Q`

5
Building Your Personal Assistant

In this chapter, we will focus our full attention on the practical side of recurrent neural networks when building a conversational chatbot. Using your most recent knowledge on sequence models, you will create an end-to-end model that aims to yield meaningful results. You will make use of a high-level TensorFlow-based library, called TensorLayer. This library makes it easier to create simple prototypes of complicated systems such as that of a chatbot. The main topics that will be covered are the following:

- **What are we building?**:This is a more detailed introduction to the exact problem and its solution
- **Preparing the data**: As always, any deep learning model requires this step, so it is crucial to mention it here
- **Creating the chatbot network**: You will learn how to use TensorLayer to build the graph for the sequence-to-sequence model used for the chatbot
- **Training the chatbot**: This step combines the data and the network graph in order to find the best possible combination of weights and biases
- **Building a conversation**: This last step uses the already trained model, together with sample sentences, to produce a meaningful conversation

What are we building?

The focus of this chapter is to walk you through building a simple conversational chatbot that is able to give answers to a set of different questions. Recently, chatbots have become more and more popular, and we can see them in numerous practical applications.

Some areas where you can see the use of this software include the following:

- **Communication between clients and businesses**, where the chatbot assists users in finding what they need, or provides support if something does not work properly. For example, Facebook offers a really handy way of implementing a chatbot for your business
- **The personal assistant behind voice control systems such as Amazon Alexa, Apple Siri, and more**: You have a full end-to-end human-like conversation where you can set reminders, order products, and more

Our simple example will present a slightly augmented version of the TensorLayer chatbot code example (`https://github.com/tensorlayer/seq2seq-chatbot`). We will be using a dataset formed of pre-collected tweets and will utilize the sequence-to-sequence model. Recall from previous chapters that this kind of model uses two recurrent neural networks, where the first one is an encoder and the second one a decoder. Later, we will give more detail on how this architecture is used for building the chatbot.

Preparing the data

In this section, we will focus on how our data (tweets, in this case) is transformed to fit the model's requirements. We will first see how, using the files in the `data/` folder from the GitHub repo for this task, the model can help us extract the needed tweets. Then, we will look at how, with the help of a simple set of functions, we can split and transform the data to achieve the needed results.

An important file to examine is `data.py`, inside the `data/twitter` folder. It transforms plain text into a numeric format so it is easy for us to train the network. We won't go deep into the implementation, since you can examine it by yourself. After running the code, we produce three important files:

- `idx_q.npy`: This is an array of arrays containing index representation of all the words in different sentences forming the chatbot questions
- `idx_a.npy`: This is an array of arrays containing index representation of all the words in different sentences forming the chatbot answers
- `metadata.pkl`: This contains both the *index to word* (`idx2w`) and *word to index* (`w2idx`) dictionaries used for this dataset

Now, let's focus on the actual usage of this data. You can review it in the first 20 lines of `ch5_task.py` from the GitHub repository for this chapter.

First, we import several Python libraries that will be used throughout the whole program:

```
import time
import tensorflow as tflow
import tensorlayer as tlayer
from sklearn.utils import shuffle
from tensorlayer.layers import EmbeddingInputlayer, Seq2Seq, DenseLayer,
retrieve_seq_length_op2
```

Here is a breakdown of these libraries, accompanied with descriptions:

- `time`: This is used for keeping track of how long our operations take. You will see its usage in the following section, where we train the network
- `tensorflow`: This is used only for a handful of operations (initializing variables, optimizing the network using adam optimizer, and initializing the TensorFlow session: `tf.Session()`)
- `tensorlayer`: As you already know, TensorLayer (`https://tensorlayer.readthedocs.io/en/stable/`) is a deep learning library on top of TensorFlow. It offers a wide range of methods and classes that make it easy for any developer to simply build solutions for complicated tasks. This library will help us construct and train our sequence-to-sequence model easily
- `shuffle`: We use this to shuffle all arrays, which represent different sentences, inside `trainX` and `trainY`. You will see how we obtain `trainX` and `trainY` in the following section
- `EmbeddingInputlayer`: A TensorLayer class that represents the input layer of a sequence-to-sequence model. As you know, every `Seq2Seq` model has two input layers, the encoder and the decoder
- `Seq2Seq`: A TensorLayer class that builds a sequence-to-sequence model similar to the one in the following diagram:

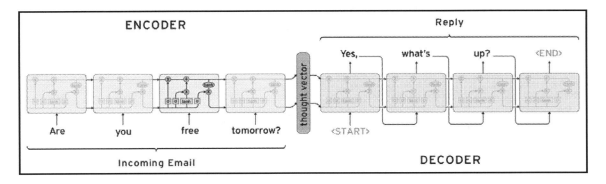

- `DenseLayer`: A TensorLayer representation of a fully connected (dense) layer. There are different types of layers that perform different transformations and are used in specific scenarios. For example, we have already used a recurrent layer, which is used for time series data. There is also a convolutional layer used for images, and so on. You can learn more about them in this video (`https://www.youtube.com/watch?v=FK77zZxaBoI`)

- `retrieve_seq_length_op2`: A TensorLayer function used for calculating the sequence length, excluding any paddings of zeros. We will use this function for both the encoding and decoding sequences

After importing the libraries, we need to access the data as follows:

```
from data.twitter import data
metadata, idx_q, idx_a = data.load_data(PATH='data/twitter/')
(trainX, trainY), (testX, testY), (validX, validY) =
data.split_dataset(idx_q, idx_a)
```

First, we load the `metadata`, `idx_q`, and `idx_a` from the `data/twitter/` folder found in the GitHub repository. Second, we use the `split_dataset` method to separate the encoder (`idx_q`) and decoder (`idx_a`) data into training (70%), testing (15%), and validation (15%).

Finally, we convert `trainX, trainY, testX, testY, validX, validY` into Python lists, and then remove the padding (zero elements) from the end of every list using a TensorLayer function, `tlayer.prepro.remove_pad_sequences()`.

Combining the preceding operations leads to well-defined training, testing, and validation data. You will see how we make use of them during training and prediction later in this chapter.

Creating the chatbot network

This section is one of the most important, so you need to make sure you understand it quite well in order to grasp the full concept of our application. We will be introducing the network graph that will be used for training and prediction.

But first, let's define the hyperparameters of the model. These are predefined constants that play a significant role in determining how well the model performs. As you will learn in the next chapter, our main task is to tweak the hyperparameters' values until we're satisfied with the model's prediction. In this case, an initial set of hyperparameters is selected. Of course, for better performance, one needs to do some optimization on them. This chapter won't focus on this part but I highly recommend doing it using techniques from the last chapter of this book (Chapter 6, *Improving Your RNN Performance*). The current hyperparameter selection is as follows:

```
batch_size = 34
embedding_dimension = 1024
learning_rate = 0.0001
number_epochs = 1000
```

Here is a brief explanation of these hyperparameters:

- batch_size: This determines how many elements each batch should have. Normally, training is done on batches where data is separated into subarrays, each with the size of batch_size
- embedding_dimension: This determines the size of the word embedding vector. A single word from the input is encoded into a vector with the size of embedding_dimension
- learning_rate: Its value determines how fast a network learns. It is typically a really small value (0.001, 0.0001). If the loss function does not decrease during training, it is good practice to reduce the learning rate
- number_epochs: This determines the number of training iterations (epochs). In the beginning of each iteration, we shuffle the data and, since an epoch is too big to feed to the computer at once, we divide it into several smaller batches. Then we train the network using these batches. After every iteration, we shuffle again and run the second epoch. This operation is done for the number of epochs we have set.

After determining the set of hyperparameters, the time comes for additional values that help us in building our model:

```
xseq_len = len(trainX)
yseq_len = len(trainY)
assert xseq_len == yseq_len

n_step = int(xseq_len/batch_size)

w2idx = metadata['w2idx']
idx2w = metadata['idx2w']
```

```
xvocab_size = len(metadata['idx2w'])
start_id = xvocab_size
end_id = xvocab_size+1

w2idx.update({'start_id': start_id})
w2idx.update({'end_id': end_id})
idx2w = idx2w + ['start_id', 'end_id']

xvocab_size = yvocab_size = xvocab_size + 2
```

Let's examine each line, one by one:

```
xseq_len = len(trainX)
yseq_len = len(trainY)
assert xseq_len == yseq_len
```

We use `xseq_len` and `yseq_len` to store the length of the encoder's and decoder's input sequence. Then, we make sure both values are equal, otherwise, the program will break.

`n_step = int(xseq_len/batch_size)`: with this, we store the number of steps that our training is about to perform. This value is only used when printing the state of training and we will see its usage later in the chapter.

We use `w2idx` and `idx2w` to store the word dictionary in both formats (the word as the dictionary key, and the ID as the dictionary key). These dictionaries are used when predicting the chatbot responses:

```
w2idx = metadata['w2idx']
idx2w = metadata['idx2w']
```

We make `start_id = xvocab_size` and `end_id = xvocab_size + 1` to assure uniqueness of these two indices. They are used for indicating the start and end of a single sentence:

```
xvocab_size = len(metadata['idx2w'])
start_id = xvocab_size
end_id = xvocab_size+1
```

Finally, we extend these dictionaries to include starting and ending elements. An example set of our data is the following:

- encode_seqs (the input encoder sentence): `['how', 'are', 'you', '<PAD_ID>']`

- decode_seqs (the input decoder sentence): `['<START_ID>', 'I', 'am', 'fine', '<PAD_ID>']`

- `target_seqs` (the predicted decoder sentence): `['I', 'am', 'fine', '<END_ID>', '<PAD_ID>']`
- `target_mask` (a mask applied at each sequence): `[1, 1, 1, 1, 0]`. This is an array the same size as `target_seqs`, but has `0` at the places where padding is applied, and `1` everywhere else. You can learn more about masking in recurrent neural networks by reading this great Quora answer (`https://www.quora.com/What-is-masking-in-a-recurrent-neural-network-RNN`)

The next step is to define our model structure. We start by introducing the model's placeholders:

```
encode_seqs = tf.placeholder(dtype=tf.int64, shape=[batch_size, None],
name="encode_seqs")
decode_seqs = tf.placeholder(dtype=tf.int64, shape=[batch_size, None],
name="decode_seqs")
target_seqs = tf.placeholder(dtype=tf.int64, shape=[batch_size, None],
name="target_seqs")
target_mask = tf.placeholder(dtype=tf.int64, shape=[batch_size, None],
name="target_mask")
```

As you can see, this is the same set of variables shown previously. Each one has a `batch_size` dimension and `tf.int64` type. Then, we calculate the model output as follows:

```
net_out, _ = model(encode_seqs, decode_seqs, is_train=True, reuse=False)
```

The purpose of the preceding line is to find the network's output using the input encoder and decoder sequences. We will define and explain the `model` method in the following section.

Finally, we define the loss function and optimizer:

```
loss = tl.cost.cross_entropy_seq_with_mask(logits=net_out.outputs,
target_seqs=target_seqs, input_mask=target_mask, name='cost')

optimizer =
tf.train.AdamOptimizer(learning_rate=learning_rate).minimize(loss)
```

As you can see, the loss function is a cross entropy with applied mask to make sure each input sequence has the same length. The `logits` (predicted outputs) are taken from the preceding model output and are accessed using `net_out.outputs`. The `target_seqs` are the expected results for every input.

The model's optimizer is `AdamOptimizer` and is defined using the built-in function from TensorFlow, `tf.train.AdamOptimizer`. As usual, we pass the `learning_rate` to decide the rate of the `loss` function minimization.

The last step is defining and explaining the `model` function:

```
def model(encode_seqs, decode_seqs, is_train=True, reuse=False):
    with tf.variable_scope("model", reuse=reuse):
        with tf.variable_scope("embedding") as vs:
            net_encode = EmbeddingInputlayer(
                inputs = encode_seqs,
                vocabulary_size = xvocab_size,
                embedding_size = embedding_dimension,
                name = 'seq_embedding')
            vs.reuse_variables()
            net_decode = EmbeddingInputlayer(
                inputs = decode_seqs,
                vocabulary_size = xvocab_size,
                embedding_size = embedding_dimension,
                name = 'seq_embedding')
        net_rnn = Seq2Seq(net_encode, net_decode,
            cell_fn = tf.contrib.rnn.BasicLSTMCell,
            n_hidden = embedding_dimension,
            initializer = tf.random_uniform_initializer(-0.1, 0.1),
            encode_sequence_length =
            retrieve_seq_length_op2(encode_seqs),
            decode_sequence_length =
            retrieve_seq_length_op2(decode_seqs),
            initial_state_encode = None,
            n_layer = 3,
            return_seq_2d = True,
            name = 'seq2seq')
        net_out = DenseLayer(net_rnn, n_units=xvocab_size,
            act=tf.identity, name='output')
    return net_out, net_rnn
```

TensorLayer makes it as simple as possible to build the sequence-to-sequence model. It uses four main components:

- `net_encode`: An encoder network using the `EmbeddingInputlayer` class.
- `net_decode`: A decoder network using the `EmbeddingInputlayer` class.
- `net_rnn`: A sequence-to-sequence model that combines the two aforementioned networks. It is implemented using the `Seq2Seq` class.
- `net_out`: The final, fully connected (dense) layer producing the end result. This layer is built on top of the sequence-to-sequence network.

net_encode and net_decode are similarly initialized using EmbeddingInputlayer (https://tensorlayer.readthedocs.io/en/stable/modules/layers.html#tensorlayer. layers.EmbeddingInputlayer). Three important parameters are used: inputs, vocabulary_size, and embedding_size. The inputs are encode_seqs or decode_seqs, which we defined in the preceding section. In both cases, vocabulary_size is equal to xvocab_size, and the embedding_size is equal to embedding_dimension. This embedding layer transforms the input vector into one of the embedding_dimension size.

net_rnn combines both the encoder and decoder layers into a full sequence-to-sequence model. The parameters are the following:

- cell_fn: The RNN cell used throughout the whole network. In our case, this is BasicLSTMCell.
- n_hidden: The number of hidden units in each of the two layers.
- initializer: The distribution used for defining the parameters (weights, biases).
- encode_sequence_length: This specifies the length of the encoder input sequence. It uses the retrieve_seq_length_op2 (https://tensorlayer. readthedocs.io/en/stable/modules/layers.html#tensorlayer.layers. retrieve_seq_length_op2) method on the encode_seqs.
- decode_sequence_length: This specifies the length of the decoder input sequence. It uses the retrive_seq_length_op2 method on the decode_seqs.
- initial_state_encode: If None, the initial state of the encoder networks is zero state and can be set automatically by the placeholder or another RNN.
- n_layer: The number of RNN layers stacked together in each of the two networks (encoder and decoder).
- return_seq_2d: If the value is True, return 2D Tensor [n_example, 2 * n_hidden], for stacking DenseLayer after it.

In the end, we use a fully connected (dense) layer net_out to calculate the final output of the network. It uses the Seq2Seq network as a previous layer, the vocabulary size (xvocab_size) as the number of units, and tf.identity as the activation function. It is normally used for explicit transport of a tensor between devices (for example, from a GPU to a CPU). In our case, we use it to build dummy nodes that copy the values from the previous layer.

One last thing to point out is the use of the `reuse` parameter and the `vs.reuse_variables()` method call. During training, we are not reusing the model's parameters (weights and biases), so `reuse = False`, but when predicting the chatbot response, we make use of the pre-trained parameters, and so have `reuse = True`. The method call triggers a reuse for the next set of calculations.

And with this, we have finished defining the model. There are only two parts left from now: training and predicting.

Training the chatbot

Once we have defined the model graph, we want to train it using our input data. Then, we will have a well-tuned set of parameters that can be used for accurate predictions.

First, we specify the TensorFlow's Session object that encapsulates the environment in which Operation (summation, subtraction, and so on) objects are executed and Tensor (placeholders, variables, and so on) objects are evaluated:

```
sess = tf.Session(config=tf.ConfigProto(allow_soft_placement=True,
log_device_placement=False))
sess.run(tf.global_variables_initializer())
```

A good explanation of the `config` parameter can be found at `https://stackoverflow.com/questions/44873273/what-do-the-options-in-configproto-like-allow-soft-placement-and-log-device-plac`. In summary, once we specify `allow_soft_placement`, the operations will be executed on the CPU only if there is no GPU registered. If this value is false, we are not allowed to execute any operation on a GPU.

Only after running the second line (`sess.run(tf.global_variables_initializer())`) will all variables actually hold their values. Initially, they only store a persistent Tensor.

Now, we will train the network using the `train()` function, defined as follows:

```
def train():
    print("Start training")
    for epoch in range(number_epochs):
        epoch_time = time.time()
        trainX_shuffled, trainY_shuffled = shuffle(trainX, trainY,
        random_state=0)
        total_err, n_iter = 0, 0

        for X, Y in tl.iterate.minibatches(inputs=trainX_shuffled,
```

```
           targets=trainY_shuffled, batch_size=batch_size, shuffle=False):

    X = tl.prepro.pad_sequences(X)

    _decode_seqs = tl.prepro.sequences_add_start_id(Y,
     start_id=start_id, remove_last=False)
    _decode_seqs = tl.prepro.pad_sequences(_decode_seqs)

    _target_seqs = tl.prepro.sequences_add_end_id(Y,
     end_id=end_id)
    _target_seqs = tl.prepro.pad_sequences(_target_seqs)
    _target_mask = tl.prepro.sequences_get_mask(_target_seqs)

    _, err = sess.run([optimizer, loss],
                          {encode_seqs: X,
                           decode_seqs: _decode_seqs,
                           target_seqs: _target_seqs,
                           target_mask: _target_mask})

    if n_iter % 200 == 0:
        print("Epoch[%d/%d] step:[%d/%d] loss:%f took:%.5fs" %
        (epoch, number_epochs, n_iter, n_step, err, time.time()
         - epoch_time))

        total_err += err; n_iter += 1
```

Let's explain what the preceding code does line by line.

The implementation has two nested loops, where the outer one decides how many times the training should go through the whole set of data. This is often done using epochs, and aims to strengthen the model accuracy. It is rarely the case that weights and biases have learned enough from a certain example when it is propagated just once. This is the reason why we should go over every example multiple times—in our case, this will be 1,000 times (the number of epochs).

After we enter an epoch iteration, we shuffle the data using the shuffle function in sklearn, which prepares it for entering the inner loop. Then, we use tl.iterate.minibatches to split the data into sub-arrays each with the batch_size size. Each iteration inside the inner loop trains the network using the current batch of data.

Before calculating the optimizer, we do some small modification on X (encoder batch data) and Y (decoder batch data). As you remember, the model has an encoder input (encoder_seqs), a decoder input (decoder_seqs), and a target output (target_seqs) incorporated into two RNNs.

The first recurrent neural network is the encoder, which accepts `encoder_seqs` as an input. In the preceding code block, this is marked with *X*. We only need to add padding to this sequence before applying it to the network. Padding is the operation of adding zeros to the end of a sequence in order for it to match a fixed length, determined by the longest sequence in the training set. This network produces a single vector which is then used in the second RNN.

The second recurrent neural network accepts the encoded vector from the first RNN and a decoder input sequence (`decoder_seqs`), and returns a predicted result. During training, we compare the predicted result to a target sequence (`target_seqs`), which happens to be the exact same sequence.

Let's clarify the preceding statement. Say you have the sentence *Hello, how are you?* as an input, and its response, *I am fine.*, as the output. The first sentence goes into the encoder network. The second sentence is the expected output of the second decoder network. We need to compare this expected output with the actual output that our decoder produces. We get the first word **I** and try to predict the following word **am**, then we get **am** and try to predict **fine**, and so on. In the beginning, our prediction will be way off, but with time, the weights and biases should be adjusted to produce accurate results. The following diagram can accompany the explanation:

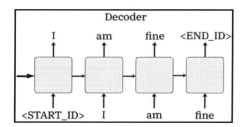

As you can see, we need to add a starting symbol to `decoder_seqs` and an ending symbol to `target_seqs`. This is what `_decode_seqs = tl.prepro.sequences_add_start_id(Y, start_id=start_id, remove_last=False)` and `_target_seqs = tl.prepro.sequences_add_end_id(Y, end_id=end_id)` do, where `start_id = xvocab_size` and `end_id = xvocab_size+1`. Finally, we add padding to both sequences, equalizing the lengths.

Just before the actual training, we extract `_target_mask` from `_target_seqs`. Recall from earlier that if `_target_seqs = ["I", "am", "fine", "<END_ID>", "<PAD_ID>"]`, then `_target_mask = [1, 1, 1, 1, 0]`.

In the end, we use the sequence arrays defined previously to train our network. It might take some time, so we have added a printing statement every 200 iterations. I would recommend leaving your computer running overnight for this training so you extract the maximum potential from your data.

The next step is to use our model in predicting an actual output. Let's see how well it can handle this task.

Building a conversation

This step is really similar to the training one. The first difference is that we don't make any evaluation of our predictions, but instead use the input to generate the results. The second difference is that we use the already trained set of variables to yield this result. You will see how it is done later in this chapter.

To make things clearer, we first initialize a new sequence-to-sequence model. Its purpose is to use the already trained weights and biases and make predictions based on different sets of inputs. We only have an encoder and decoder sequence, where the encoder one is an input sentence and the decoder sequence is fed one word at a time. We define the new model as follows:

```
encode_seqs2 = tf.placeholder(dtype=tf.int64, shape=[1, None],
name="encode_seqs")
decode_seqs2 = tf.placeholder(dtype=tf.int64, shape=[1, None],
name="decode_seqs")
net, net_rnn = model(encode_seqs2, decode_seqs2, is_train=False,
reuse=True)
y = tf.nn.softmax(net.outputs)
```

As you can see, it follows exactly the same pattern as the training architecture, with the difference that our sequence matrices are of shape 1, instead of `batch_size`.

An important thing to note is that when calculating the network's results, we must **reuse** the same parameters used during training. This step is essential because it makes sure our prediction is a result of the recent training we have done.

Finally, we calculate the final output, y, using the softmax function. This is usually done at the final layer to make sure that our vector values sum up to 1, and is a necessary step during classification.

After defining our new model, the time comes for the actual prediction. We follow this pattern:

1. Generate an initial sentence that will start the conversation.
2. Convert the sentence into a list of word indices using the word2idx dictionary.
3. Decide how many replies back and forth we want the conversation to have (in our case, this would be five).
4. Calculate the final state of the encoder by feeding the net_rnn (as defined previously) with the initial sentence.
5. Finally, we iteratively predict the next word using the previously predicted word and the network. At the first time step, we use start_id, as defined previously, as the first word from the decoder.

These steps are executed in the following code snippet:

```python
def predict():
    seeds = ["happy birthday have a nice day",
            "the presidential debate held last night was spectacular"]
    for seed in seeds:
        seed_id = [w2idx[w] for w in seed.split(" ")]
        for _ in range(5):  # 5 Replies
            # 1. encode, get state
            state = sess.run(net_rnn.final_state_encode,
                        {encode_seqs2: [seed_id]})

            # 2. decode, feed start_id, get first word
            o, state = sess.run([y, net_rnn.final_state_decode],
                        {net_rnn.initial_state_decode: state,
                        decode_seqs2: [[start_id]]})

            w_id = tl.nlp.sample_top(o[0], top_k=3)
            w = idx2w[w_id]

            # 3. decode, feed state iteratively
            sentence = [w]
            for _ in range(30): # max sentence length
                o, state = sess.run([y, net_rnn.final_state_decode],
                            {net_rnn.initial_state_decode: state,
                            decode_seqs2: [[w_id]]})
                w_id = tl.nlp.sample_top(o[0], top_k=2)
                w = idx2w[w_id]
```

```
        if w_id == end_id:
            break
        sentence = sentence + [w]

    print(" >", ' '.join(sentence))
```

An interesting thing to note is how `# 2. decode, feed start_id, get first word` and `# 3. decode, feed state iteratively` perform exactly the same action, but step #2 is a special case, focused on predicting only the first word. Step #3 uses this first word to iteratively predict all the others.

`tl.nlp.sample_top(o[0], top_k=3)` might also be confusing to you. This line samples an index from the probability array o[0], where you consider only three candidates. The same functionality goes for `w_id = tl.nlp.sample_top(o[0], top_k = 2)`. You can learn more on the TensorLayer documentation (`https://tensorlayer.readthedocs.io/en/stable/modules/nlp.html#sampling-functions`).

Finally, we print the formed sentence of 30 words (we cap the number of words per sentence). If you trained the network long enough, you should see some decent results. If they don't satisfy you, then extensive work is needed. You will learn more about this in the upcoming `Chapter 6`, *Improving Your RNN Performance*.

Summary

This chapter reveals a full implementation of a chatbot system that manages to construct a short conversation. The prototype shows, in detail, each stage of building the intelligent chatbot. This includes collecting data, training the network, and making predictions (generating conversation).

For the network's architecture, we use the powerful encoder-decoder sequence-to-sequence model that utilizes two recurrent neural networks, while connecting them using an encoder vector. For the actual implementation, we make use of a deep learning library built on top of TensorFlow, called TensorLayer. It simplifies most of the work by introducing simple one-line implementations of standard models such as *sequence-to sequence*. In addition, this library is useful for preprocessing your data before using it for training.

The next chapter shifts focus to, probably, the most important part of building a recurrent neural network (and any deep learning model), which is how to improve your performance and actually make your program return satisfying results. As you have already seen, building a neural network follows a similar pattern in most basic/medium examples. The hard part is to make sure the implementations are actually useful and produce meaningful results. This will be the focus of our next chapter—I hope you enjoy it.

External links

- TensorLayer chatbot code example: https://github.com/tensorlayer/seq2seq-chatbot
- TensorLayer library: https://tensorlayer.readthedocs.io/en/stable/
- Layers in neural network: https://www.youtube.com/watch?v=FK77zZxaBoI
- What is masking in a recurrent neural network (RNN)?: https://www.quora.com/What-is-masking-in-a-recurrent-neural-network-RNN
- TensorLayer's embeddingInputlayer class: https://tensorlayer.readthedocs.io/en/stable/modules/layers.html#tensorlayer.layers.EmbeddingInputlayer
- TensorLayer's retrieve_seq_length_op2 method: https://tensorlayer.readthedocs.io/en/stable/modules/layers.html#tensorlayer.layers.retrieve_seq_length_op2
- TensorFlow session's config parameter: https://stackoverflow.com/questions/44873273/what-do-the-options-in-configproto-like-allow-soft-placement-and-log-device-plac
- TensorLayer Sampling Functions: https://tensorlayer.readthedocs.io/en/stable/modules/nlp.html#sampling-functions

6
Improving Your RNN Performance

This chapter goes through some techniques for improving your recurrent neural network model. Often, the initial results from your model can be disappointing, so you need to find ways of improving them. This can be done with various methods and tools, but we will focus on two main areas:

- Improving the RNN model performance with data and tuning
- Optimizing the TensorFlow library for better results

First, we will see how more data, as well as tuning the hyperparameters, can yield significantly better results. Then our focus will shift to getting the most out of the built-in TensorFlow functionality. Both approaches are applicable to any task that involves the neural network model, so the next time you want to do image recognition with convolutional networks or fix a rescaled image with GAN, you can apply the same techniques for perfecting your model.

Improving your RNN model

When working on a problem using RNN (or any other network), your process looks like this:

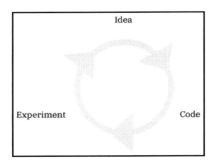

First, you come up with an **idea for the model**, its hyperparameters, the number of layers, how deep the network should be, and so on. Then the model is **implemented and trained** in order to produce some results. Finally, these results are **assessed** and the necessary modifications are made. It is rarely the case that you'll receive meaningful results from the first run. This cycle may occur multiple times until you are satisfied with the outcome.

Considering this approach, one important question comes to mind: *How can we change the model so the next cycle produces better results?*

This question is tightly connected to your understanding of the network's results. Let's discuss that now.

As you already know, in the beginning of each model training, you need to prepare lots of quality data. This step should happen before the **Idea** part of the aforementioned cycle. Then, during the **Idea** stage, you should come up with the actual neural network and its characteristics. After that comes the **Code** stage, where you use your data to supply the model and perform the actual training. There is something important to keep in mind—*once your data is collected, you need to split it into 3 parts: training (80%), validation (10%) and testing (10%)*.

The **Code** stage only uses the training part of your data. Then, the **Experiment** stage uses the validation part to evaluate the model. Based on the results of these two operations, we will make the necessary changes.

You should use the testing data **only** after you have gone through all the necessary cycles and have identified that your model is performing well. The testing data will help you understand the rate of accuracy you are receiving on unseen data.

At the end of each cycle, you need to determine how good your model is. Based on the results, you will see that your model is always either **underfitting (high bias)** or **overfitting (high variance)** the data (by varying degrees). You should aim for both the bias and variance to be low, so there is almost no underfitting or overfitting. The next diagram may help you understand this concept better:

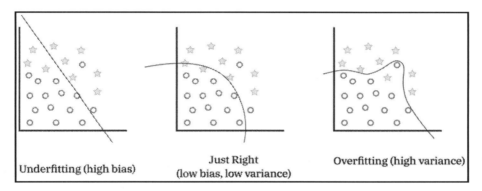

Examining the preceding diagram, we can state the following definitions:

- **Underfitting (high bias)**: This occurs when the network is not influenced enough by the training data, and generalizes the prediction
- **Just Right (low bias, low variance)**: This occurs when the network makes quality predictions, both during training and in the general case during testing
- **Overfitting (high variance)**: This occurs when the network is influenced by the training data too much, and makes false decisions on new entries.

The preceding diagram may be helpful to understand the concepts of high bias and high variance, but it is difficult to apply this to real examples. The problem is that we normally deal with data of more than two dimensions. That is why we will be using the loss (error) function values produced by the model to make the same evaluation for higher dimensional data.

Let's say we are evaluating the Spanish-to-English translator neural network from Chapter 4, *Creating a Spanish-to-English Translator*. We can assume that the lowest possible error on that task can be produced by a human, and it is 1.5%. Now we will evaluate the results based on all the error combinations that our network can give:

- Training data error: ~2%; Validation data error: ~14%: **high variance**
- Training data error: ~14%; Validation data error: ~15%: **high bias**
- Training data error: ~14%; Validation data error: ~30%: **high variance, high bias**
- Training data error:~2%; Validation data error: ~2.4%: **low variance, low bias**

The desired output is having low variance and low bias. Of course, it takes a lot of time and effort to get this kind of improvement, but in the end, it is worth doing.

You have now got familiar with how to read your model results and evaluate the model's performance. Now, let's see what can be done to **lower both the variance and the bias of the model**.

How can we lower the variance? (fixing overfitting)

A very useful approach is to collect and transform more data. This will generalize the model and make it perform well on both the training and validation sets.

How can we lower the bias? (fixing underfitting)

This can be done by increasing the network depth—that is, changing the numbers of layers and of hidden units, and tuning the hyperparameters.

Next, we will cover both of these approaches and see how to use them effectively to improve our neural network's performance.

Improving performance with data

A large amount of quality data is critical for the success of any deep learning model. A good comparison can be made to other algorithms, where an increased volume of data does not necessarily improve performance:

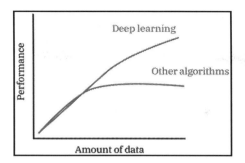

But this doesn't mean that gathering more data is always the right approach. For example, if our model suffers from underfitting, more data won't increase the performance. On the other hand, solving the overfitting problem can be done using exactly that approach.

Improving the model performance with data comes in three steps: **selecting data**, **processing data**, and **transforming data**. It is important to note that all three steps should be done according to your specific problem. For some tasks, such as recognizing digits inside an image, a nicely formatted dataset can be found easily. For more concrete tasks (e.g. analyzing images from plants), you may need to experiment and come up with non-trivial decisions.

Selecting data

This is a pretty straightforward technique. You either collect more data or invent more training examples.

Finding more data can be done using an online collection of datasets (https://skymind.ai/wiki/open-datasetshttps://skymind.ai/wiki/open-datasets). Other methods are to scrape web pages, or use the advanced options of Google Search (https://www.google.com/advanced_search).

On the other hand, inventing or augmenting data is a challenging and complex problem, especially if we are trying to generate text or images. For example, a new approach (https://www.quora.com/What-data-augmentation-techniques-are-available-for-deep-learning-on-text) for augmenting text was created recently. It is done by translating an English sentence to another language and then back to English. This way we are getting two slightly different but meaningful sentences, which increases and diversifies our dataset substantially. Another interesting technique for augmenting data, specifically for RNN language models, can be found in the paper on *Data Noising as Smoothing in Neural Network Language Models* (https://arxiv.org/abs/1703.02573).

Processing data

After you have selected the required data, the time comes for processing. This can be done with these three steps:

- **Formatting**: This involves converting the data into the most suitable format for your application. Imagine, for example, that your data is the text from thousands of PDF files. You should extract the text and covert the data into CSV format.
- **Cleaning**: Often, it is the case that your data may be incomplete. For example, if you have scraped book metadata from the internet, some entries may have missing data (such as ISBN, date of writing, and so on). Your job is to decide whether to fix or discard the metadata for the whole book.
- **Sampling**: Using a small part of the dataset can reduce computational time and speed up your training cycles while you are determining the model accuracy.

The order of the preceding steps is not determined, and you may revisit them multiple times.

Transforming data

Finally, you need to transform the data using techniques such as scaling, decomposition, and feature selection. First, it is good to plot/visualize your data using Matplotlib (a Python library) or TensorFlow's TensorBoard (https://www.tensorflow.org/guide/summaries_and_tensorboard).

Scaling is a technique that converts every entry into a number within a specific range (0-1) without mitigating its effectiveness. Normally, scaling is done within the bounds of your activation functions. If you are using sigmoid activation functions, rescale your data to values between 0 and 1. If you're using the hyperbolic tangent (tanh), rescale to values between -1 and 1. This applies to inputs (x) and outputs (y).

Decomposition is a technique of splitting some features into their components and using them instead. For example, the feature time may have minutes and hours, but we care only about the minutes.

Feature selection is one of the most important decisions you would make when building your model. A great tutorial to follow when deciding how to choose the most appropriate features is Jason Brownlee's *An Introduction to Feature Selection* (https://machinelearningmastery.com/an-introduction-to-feature-selection/).

Processing and transforming data can be accomplished using the vast selection of Python libraries, such as NumPy, among others. They turn out to be pretty handy when it comes to data manipulation.

After you have gone through all of the preceding steps (probably multiple times), you can move forward to building your neural network model.

Improving performance with tuning

After selecting, processing, and transforming your data, it's time for a second optimization technique—hyperparameter tuning. This approach is one of the most important components in building your model and you need to spend the time necessary to execute it well.

Every neural network model has parameters and hyperparameters. These are two distinct sets of values. Parameters are learned by the model during training, such as weights and biases. On the other hand, hyperparameters are predefined values that are selected after careful observation. In a standard recurrent neural network, the set of hyperparameters includes the number of hidden units, number of layers, RNN model type, sequence length, batch size, number of epochs (iterations), and the learning rate.

Your task is to identify the best of all possible combinations so that the network performs pretty well. This is a pretty challenging task and often takes a lot of time (hours, days, even months) and computational power.

Following Andrew Ng's tutorial on hyperparameter tuning (https://www.coursera.org/lecture/deep-neural-network/hyperparameters-tuning-in-practice-pandas-vs-caviar-DHNcc), we can separate this process into two different techniques: *Pandas* vs *Caviar*.

The *Pandas* approach follows the way pandas (that is, the animal) raise their children. We initialize our model with a specific set of parameters, and then improve these values after every training operation until we achieve delightful results. This approach is ideal if you lack computational power and multiple GPUs to train neural networks simultaneously.

The *Caviar* approach follows the way fish reproduce. We introduce multiple models at once (using different sets of parameters) and train them at the same time, while tracking the results. This technique will likely require access to more computational power.

Now the question becomes: *How can we decide what should be included in our set of hyperparameters?*

Summarizing a great article on hyperparameters optimization (http://neupy.com/2016/ 12/17/hyperparameter_optimization_for_neural_networks.html#tree-structured- parzen-estimators-tpe), we can define five ways for tuning:

- **Grid search**
- **Random search**
- **Hand-tuning**
- **Bayesian optimization**
- **Tree-structured Parzen Estimators** (TPE)

During the beginning phase of your deep learning journey, you will mostly be utilizing grid search, random search, and hand-tuning. The last two techniques are more complex in terms of understanding and implementation. We will cover both of them in the following section, but bear in mind that, for trivial tasks, you can go with normal hand-tuning.

Grid search

This is the most straightforward way of finding the right hyperparameters. It follows the approach in this graph:

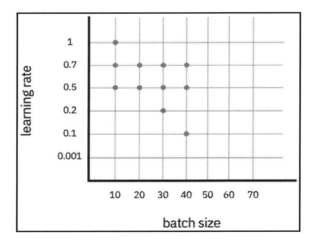

Here, we generate all the possible combinations of values for the hyperparameters and perform separate training cycles. This works for small neural networks, but is impractical for more complex tasks. That is why we should use the better approach listed in the following section.

Random search

This technique is similar to grid search. You can follow the graph here:

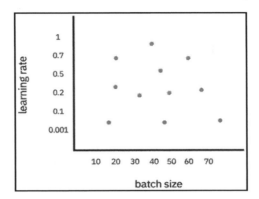

Instead of taking all the possible combinations, we sample a smaller set of random values and use these values to train the model. If we see that a particular group of closely positioned dots tends to perform better, we can examine this region more closely and focus on it.

Hand-tuning

Bigger networks normally require more time for training. This is why the aforementioned approaches are not ideal for such situations. In these cases, we often use the hand-tuning technique. The idea is to initially try one set of values, and then evaluate the performance. Then, our intuition, as well as our learning experience, may lead to ideas on a specific sequence of changes. We perform those tweaks and learn new things about the model. After several iterations, we have a good understanding of what needs to change for future improvement.

Bayesian optimization

This approach is a way of learning the hyperparameters without the need to manually determine different values. It uses a Gaussian process that utilizes a set of previously evaluated parameters, and the resultant accuracy, to make an assumption about unobserved parameters. An acquisition function uses this information to suggest the next set of parameters. For more information, I suggest watching Professor Hinton's lecture on *Bayesian optimization of Hyper Parameters* (https://www.youtube.com/watch?v=cWQDeB9WqvU).

Tree-structured Parzen Estimators (TPE)

The idea behind this approach is that, at each iteration, TPE collects new observations, and at the end of the iteration, the algorithm decides which set of parameters it should try next. For more information, I suggest taking a look at this amazing article on *Hyperparameters optimization for Neural Networks* (`http://neupy.com/2016/12/17/ hyperparameter_optimization_for_neural_networks.html#tree-structured-parzen-estimators-tpe`).

Optimizing the TensorFlow library

This section focuses mostly on practical advice that can be directly implemented in your code. The TensorFlow team has provided a large set of tools that can be utilized to improve your performance. These techniques are constantly being updated to achieve better results. I strongly recommend watching TensorFlow's video on training performance from the 2018 TensorFlow conference (`https://www.youtube.com/watch?v=SxOsJPaxHME`). This video is accompanied by nicely aggregated documentation, which is also a must-read (`https:// www.tensorflow.org/performance/`).

Now, let's dive into more details around what you can do to achieve faster and more reliable training.

Let's first start with an illustration from TensorFlow that presents the general steps of training a neural network. You can divide this process into three phases: **data processing, performing training**, and **optimizing gradients**:

1. **Data processing (step 1)**: This phase includes fetching the data (locally or from a network) and transforming it to fit our needs. These transformations might include augmentation, batching, and so on. Normally, these operations are done on the **CPU**.
2. **Perform training (steps 2a, 2b and 2c)**: This phase includes computing the forward pass during training, which requires a specific neural network model—LSTM, GPU, or a basic RNN in our case. These operations utilize powerful **GPUs** and **TPUs**.
3. **Optimize gradients (step 3)**: This phase includes the process of minimizing the loss function with the aim of optimizing the weights. The operation is again performed on **GRUs** and **TPUs**.

This graph illustrates the above steps:

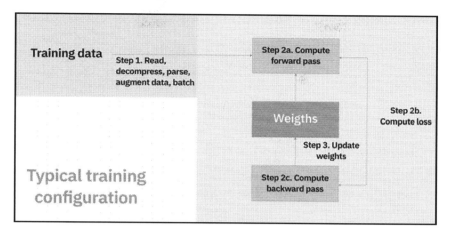

Next, let's explain how to improve each of these steps.

Data processing

You need to examine if loading and transforming the data is the bottleneck of your performance. You can do this with several approaches, some of which involve estimating the time it takes to perform these tasks, as well as tracking the CPU usage.

After you have determined that these operations are slowing down the performance of your model, it's time to apply some useful techniques to speed things up.

As we said, these operations (loading and transforming data) should be performed on the CPU, rather than the GPU, so that you free up the latter for training. To ensure this, wrap your code as follows:

```
with tf.device('/cpu:0'):
    # call a function that fetches and transforms the data
    final_data = fetch_and_process_data()
```

Then, you need to focus on both the process of loading (fetching) and transforming the data.

Improving data loading

The TensorFlow team has been working hard to make this as easy as possible by providing the `tf.data` API (`https://www.tensorflow.org/performance/performance_guide`), which works incredibly well. To learn more about it and understand how to use it efficiently, I recommend watching TensorFlow's talk on `tf.data` (`https://www.youtube.com/watch?v=uIcqeP7MFH0`). This API should always be used, instead of the standard `feed_dict` approach you have seen so far.

Improving data transformation

Transformations can come in different forms, for example, cropping images, splitting text, and rendering and batching files. TensorFlow offers solutions for these techniques. For example, if you are cropping images before training, it is good to use `tf.image.decode_and_crop_jpeg`, which decodes only the part of the image required. Another optimization can be made in the batching process. The TensorFlow library offers two methods:

```
batch_normalization = tf.layers.batch_normalization(input_layer,
fused=True, data_format='NCHW')
```

The second method is as follows:

```
batch_normalizaton = tf.contrib.layers.batch_norm(input_layer, fused=True,
data_format='NCHW')
```

Let's clarify these lines:

- Batch normalization is performed to a neural network model to speed up the process of training. Refer to this amazing article, *Batch Normalization in Neural Networks*, for more details: `https://towardsdatascience.com/batch-normalization-in-neural-networks-1ac91516821c`.
- The `fused` parameter indicates whether or not the method should combine the multiple operations, required for batch normalization, into a single kernel.
- The `data_format` parameter refers to the structure of the Tensor passed to a given Operation (such as summation, division, training, and so on). A good explanation can be found under *Data formats* in the TensorFlow performance guide (`https://www.tensorflow.org/performance/`).

Performing the training

Now, let's move on to the phase of performing the training. Here, we are using one of TensorFlow's built-in functions for initializing recurrent neural network cells and calculating their weights using the preprocessed data.

Depending on your situation, different techniques for optimizing your training may be more appropriate:

- For small and experimental models, you can use `tf.nn.rnn_cell.BasicLSTMCell`. Unfortunately, this is highly inefficient and takes up more memory than the following optimized versions. That is why using it is **not** recommended, unless you are just experimenting.
- An optimized version of the previous code is `tf.contrib.rnn.LSTMBlockFusedCell`. It should be used when you don't have access to GPUs or TPUs and want run a more efficient cell.
- The best set of cells to use is under `tf.contrib.cudnn_rnn.*` (`CuddnnCompatibleGPUCell` for GPU cells and more). They are highly optimized to run on GPUs and perform significantly better than the preceding ones.

Finally, you should always perform the training using `tf.nn.dynamic_rnn` (see the TensorFlow documentation: `https://www.tensorflow.org/api_docs/python/tf/nn/dynamic_rnn`) and pass the specific cell. This method optimizes the training of the recurrent neural networks by occasionally swapping memory between GPUs and CPUs to enable training of large sequences.

Optimizing gradients

The last optimization technique will actually improve the performance of our backpropagation algorithm. Recall from the previous chapters that your goal during training is to minimize the loss function by adjusting the weights and biases of the model. Adjusting (optimizing) these weights and biases can be accomplished with different built-in TensorFlow optimizers, such as `tf.train.AdamOptimizer` and `tf.train.GradientDescentOptimizer`.

TensorFlow offers the ability to distribute this process across multiple TPUs using this code:

```
optimizer = tf.contrib.tpu.CrossShardOptimizer(existing_optimizer)
```

Here, `existing_optimizer = tf.train.AdamOptimizer()`, and your training step will look like `train_step = optimizer.minimize(loss)`.

Summary

In this chapter, we covered a lot of new and exciting approaches for optimizing your model's performance, both on a general level, and specifically, using the TensorFlow library.

The first part covered techniques for improving your RNN performance by selecting, processing, and transforming your data, as well as tuning your hyperparameters. You also learned how to understand your model in more depth, and now know what should be done to make it work better.

The second part was specifically focused on practical ways of improving your model's performance using the built-in TensorFlow functions. The team at TensorFlow seeks to make it as easy as possible for you to quickly achieve the results you want by providing distributed environments and optimization techniques with just a few lines of code.

Combining both of the techniques covered in this chapter will enhance your knowledge in deep learning and let you experiment with more complicated models without worrying about performance issues. The knowledge you gained is applicable for any neural network model, so you can confidently apply exactly the same technique for broader sets of problems.

External links

- Open source data collection: `https://skymind.ai/wiki/open-datasets` or awesome-public-datasets GitHub repo: `https://github.com/awesomedata/awesome-public-datasets`
- Google Search Advanced: `https://www.google.com/advanced_search`
- Augmenting text: `https://www.quora.com/What-data-augmentation-techniques-are-available-for-deep-learning-on-text`
- Data Noising as Smoothing in Neural Network Language Models: `https://arxiv.org/abs/1703.02573`
- TensorBoard: `https://www.tensorflow.org/guide/summaries_and_tensorboard`
- An Introduction to Feature Selection: `https://machinelearningmastery.com/an-introduction-to-feature-selection/`
- Andrew Ng's course on hyperparameters tuning: `https://www.coursera.org/lecture/deep-neural-network/hyperparameters-tuning-in-practice-pandas-vs-caviar-DHNcc`
- Hyperparameters optimization for Neural Networks: `http://neupy.com/2016/12/17/hyperparameter_optimization_for_neural_networks.html#tree-structured-parzen-estimators-tpe`
- Bayesian Optimization of Hyper Parameters: `https://www.youtube.com/watch?v=cWQDeB9WqvU`
- Training performance (TensorFlow Summit 2018): `https://www.youtube.com/watch?v=SxOsJPaxHME`
- TensorFlow Performance Guide: `https://www.tensorflow.org/performance/`
- tf.data API: `https://www.tensorflow.org/performance/performance_guide`
- `tf.data` (TensorFlow Summit 2018): `https://www.youtube.com/watch?v=uIcqeP7MFH0`
- Batch Normalization in Neural Networks: `https://towardsdatascience.com/batch-normalization-in-neural-networks-1ac91516821c`

Other Books You May Enjoy

If you enjoyed this book, you may be interested in these other books by Packt:

Advanced Deep Learning with Keras
Rowel Atienza

ISBN: 978-1-78862-941-6

- Cutting-edge techniques in human-like AI performance
- Implement advanced deep learning models using Keras
- The building blocks for advanced techniques - MLPs, CNNs, and RNNs
- Deep neural networks – ResNet and DenseNet
- Autoencoders and Variational AutoEncoders (VAEs)
- Generative Adversarial Networks (GANs) and creative AI techniques
- Disentangled Representation GANs, and Cross-Domain GANs
- Deep Reinforcement Learning (DRL) methods and implementation
- Produce industry-standard applications using OpenAI gym
- Deep Q-Learning and Policy Gradient Methods

Deep Learning Quick Reference
Mike Bernico

ISBN: 978-1-78883-799-6

- Solve regression and classification challenges with TensorFlow and Keras
- Learn to use Tensor Board for monitoring neural networks and its training
- Optimize hyperparameters and safe choices/best practices
- Build CNN's, RNN's, and LSTM's and using word embedding from scratch
- Build and train seq2seq models for machine translation and chat applications.
- Understanding Deep Q networks and how to use one to solve an autonomous agent problem.
- Explore Deep Q Network and address autonomous agent challenges.

Leave a review - let other readers know what you think

Please share your thoughts on this book with others by leaving a review on the site that you bought it from. If you purchased the book from Amazon, please leave us an honest review on this book's Amazon page. This is vital so that other potential readers can see and use your unbiased opinion to make purchasing decisions, we can understand what our customers think about our products, and our authors can see your feedback on the title that they have worked with Packt to create. It will only take a few minutes of your time, but is valuable to other potential customers, our authors, and Packt. Thank you!

Index

Made in the USA
San Bernardino, CA
07 February 2019